Breaking into the Current

BOATWOMEN OF THE GRAND CANYON

Breaking into the Current

Louise Teal

The University of Arizona Press
Tucson & London

The University of Arizona Press

∞ This book is printed on acid-free, archival-quality paper.
Manufactured in the United States of America

98 97 96 95 94 5 4 3 2 1

Library of Congress Cataloging-in-Publication Data

Teal, Louise, 1946-
Breaking into the current : boatwomen of the Grand Canyon / Louise Teal.
p. cm.
Includes bibliographical references.
ISBN 0-8165-1413-5 (cl. : alk. paper).—
ISBN 0-8165-1429-1 (pbk. : alk. paper)
1. Boating for women. 2. Boats and boating—Colorado River (Colo.-Mexico)—History. 3. Pilots and pilotage—United States—Interviews. 4. Women—United States—Recreation—Interviews. I. Title.
GV777.57.T43 1994 93-35400
797.1'09791'3—dc20 CIP

British Cataloguing-in-Publication Data
A catalogue record for this book is available from the British Library.

To all women
navigating the changing currents
of our time

Contents

Illustrations

Preface

"I made no bones about it. I put the Canyon first; I put it before anything," said Georgie White, the first boatwoman to guide commercial passengers downriver through the Grand Canyon. Her feelings would be echoed by many women who followed her. We would all like to have explored the Canyon when she did—to have seen the Indian ruins littered with pottery and to have felt the flow of the Colorado River before Glen Canyon Dam turned the downstream temperature to ice.

Georgie's love affair with the Colorado began back in 1945, when she and her friend, Harry Aleson, hiked into the Canyon's remote lower gorge, jumped into the muddy swirling flood waters, and swam downriver for four days. In 1952, when she was forty-one years old, she became the "first woman to handle oars all the way through the Grand Canyon."[1] By 1955, she had pioneered her giant G-rigs—huge inflatable boats designed to safely motor large groups through the Canyon's 160 rapids—some of the biggest and noisiest white water in North America.

After Georgie's first Canyon trip, twenty years passed

1. David Lavender, *River Runners of the Grand Canyon*, p. 114.

before another woman worked as a Grand Canyon commercial river guide. By the early 1970s, women were working as river guides in other parts of the country on smaller, more technically difficult rivers. But the Grand Canyon, with the exception of Georgie, seemed to be reserved for male river guides—big place, big boats, big water. As the years passed, quite a few women began breaking into this current and running motor and oar boats down the Colorado's rapids.

Much has been written about Georgie and rightfully so: she was a pioneer and a legend.[2] But there have been other boatwomen in the Canyon since, women whose greatest love has been the river that glides, churns, and explodes through one of the most majestic canyons in the world.

These pages are for them.

I spent a good part of 1990 and 1991 collecting the feelings, thoughts, and memories of more than forty women who work or had worked as Grand Canyon commercial river guides. By that time, approximately 16 percent of an estimated 275 full-season guides in charge of boats were women. When I started rowing in 1974, you could count the women guides working for the twenty different companies on one hand.

Along with the written history about the Canyon, a rich oral tradition exists among boat guides—each river mile swirls with its own memories. I wish there was room for all the stories and characters I wanted to include, credit, and

2. Publications about Georgie include Rose Marie DeRoss, *Adventures of Georgie White, TV's "Woman of the Rivers"* (Costa Mesa: Gardner Printing and Mailing Co., 1958) and Georgie White Clark and Duane Newcomb, *Georgie Clark: Thirty Years of River Running* (San Francisco: Chronicle Books, 1977), as well as many magazine articles.

honor. Instead, it seemed best to narrow the focus—to profile eleven of the early guides who laid the groundwork for women working and whose stories, taken as a whole, could represent various types of boatwomen and their passion for the Grand Canyon. This book portrays eleven of the first full-season boatwomen after Georgie, beginning with the four earliest, who started running commercial passengers in 1973 and 1974. In 1976, more women began running boats, and the next seven women profiled, in chronological order, began running passengers in the middle-to-late 1970s. I chose to include them for a combination of reasons: they either still worked in the Canyon, had worked the most trips, or had led trips.

The introductory chapters provide a brief history of river running in the Grand Canyon, especially as it pertains to women, plus a glimpse of the river journey's environment. A later chapter after the stories of the earliest guides focuses on one spectacular high-water year, a year when most of the women portrayed in this book were on the water. The last chapter is devoted to certain sexism issues—although there were many men who welcomed women working on the river, there were some who did not.

Each of the profile chapters describes a different woman, but each woman also tells a part of every Canyon boatwoman's story. When Marilyn Sayre talks about wanting to quit, when Ellen Tibbets talks about crew camaraderie, when Susan Billingsley talks about adventure in wild country, when Sue Bassett talks about her mission, when Lorna Corson talks about winter worries, when Martha Clark talks about the thrill of white water—in a very real sense, these women speak for us all. We were all in the same romance. Through these women, I hope I have created a composite picture of Grand Canyon boatwomen that honors all past and present women of the river.

And that honors all women. While these boatwomen made a career choice that may seem thrilling and unusual, they were only following their hearts amidst the pressures and possibilities facing all women in our particular era.

Breaking into the Current

CHAPTER 1

Women in the Canyon

"Hey, you hags, are the boats unloaded yet?"

Lorna and I turned to see another boatman grinning up at us. "Sure," we said, laughing. "Here, catch these!" and within seconds he was dodging flying gear bags.

The nickname "hags" sounds grating to most people, but the women who row for one river company use it with affection. To us, it symbolizes the feel of our oars pulling through water, the sweet comfort and awesome beauty of five-thousand-foot cliffs, the roar of rapids, and the laughter of our passengers. To us, being a hag means being a woman river guide on commercial trips through the Grand Canyon.

It can also mean working long hours. No matter which company a boatwoman works for, she doesn't punch out at five o'clock each day during the 225-mile trips that last eight to eighteen days. Sometimes we row against seemingly endless upstream winds. Our skin is dried out by too much sun, and our brains are fried by hundred-degree heat. We face other assaults on our bodies, the latest being some incurable form of foot rot. But for the six-month river season, these minor irritations are more than offset by watching that massive pile of rock, the Grand Canyon, work its particular magic on folks.

And then there's the River. . .

The Grand Canyon owes its creation primarily to a river's journey through the slow-rising plateau of northern Arizona, a process that began some forty million years ago. When Spanish explorers saw this hardworking silty river, they named it El Rio Colorado, or the red river. The Colorado's headwaters run clear as they tumble out of the Rocky Mountains. The river has grown large and muddy by the time it meets the Green River, deep in Utah's Canyonlands National Park. There, the Colorado gathers waters from Wyoming's Wind River Mountains and Utah's Uinta Mountains. As the river continues to carve and twist its way to the Gulf of California, it creates several desert canyons, but the best known, the grandest of them all, is the Grand Canyon. Southwesterners, no strangers to magnificent canyons, usually refer to it as *the* Canyon. The sculpting of the Canyon begins in northeastern Arizona below Lee's Ferry, a river crossing that was discovered by a Mormon scout in 1858 and was the best river crossing along a desolate 500-mile stretch of the Colorado's canyons until Navajo Bridge was finished in 1928. The river carves south from Lee's Ferry for sixty-one miles and then turns, cutting its way west. Two hundred and seventy-six twisting miles after the Colorado flows past Lee's Ferry, it emerges from the Grand Canyon. In the Canyon's depths, more than a mile below the forested rim, the river sculpts and polishes two-billion-year-old rock. Throughout the Canyon, perpendicular to the river and usually following fault lines, rain has eroded back smaller drainages, or side canyons. Together, rain and river waters have designed one of the deepest, most expansive, beautiful labyrinths of canyons in the world—and one of the last places in the United States to be explored and mapped by "modern" man.

Before Georgie White rowed her first boat through the

David Edwards. Color slide.

Georgie White

Grand Canyon, boats running the Colorado may have had women's names, but never women pilots. Back in 1869, John Wesley Powell commanded the wooden "Emma Dean" on his exploration of the Grand Canyon. Twenty years later, Robert Brewster Stanton's expedition rode downriver on the "Sweet Marie" and the "Bonnie Jean," as the crew surveyed the Canyon for a railway route west.

Previous to Powell's expedition, history records two other Grand Canyon river journeys—one planned, one unplanned. Hopi legends tell of a young man who, riding in a hollowed-out log and using a magic wand to maneuver, floated through the Canyon and on out to the sea. In September of 1887, prospector James White allegedly rode through the Canyon on a makeshift log raft, hastily put together to escape attacking Indians on the upper Colorado. Controversy still rages as to whether White actually made the journey.

No one denies Powell the credit for being the first white man to lead a planned expedition through the Grand Canyon. His wooden boats put on the water up in Green River, Wyoming. When they encountered rapids, the oarsmen, their backs facing downstream, rowed like crazy while the stern man shouted commands and ruddered. (In 1897, trapper Nathaniel Galloway developed the rowing technique prevalent in rapids today—only one oarman rowing and facing downstream. But when it is time to make a powerful cut across the water, modern oarsmen and women still turn their backs downstream and row like crazy.) Like many expeditions that were to follow, Powell's men lined or portaged the worst rapids. *Lining* meant trying to control the boats by rope from shore; *portaging* meant unloading supplies and carrying the heavy boats around the rapid. Both techniques involved back-breaking labor. Powell's trip met with misfortune, hunger, and desertion, but three months after his party started, it emerged from the depths of the Canyon.

During the next sixty years, more adventurers ran the rapids of the Colorado, hoping to make their fortunes from recording or retelling their adventures. That was the intent of Glen and Bessie Hyde, who spent their honeymoon in 1928 floating through the Canyon, or almost all the way through. After they failed to arrive at their planned destination, a search party found their empty flat-bottomed wooden scow bobbing near shore, with its bowline wedged between two rocks, just thirty-nine miles short of the end of the Canyon. What happened to the honeymooners has remained a mystery to this day. Unclear, too, is how often Bessie handled the sweep oars attached to the bow and stern of their twenty-five-foot scow. In any case, what with unplanned swims, repairs, and lining rapids, the trip must have been a physical ordeal for them both.

The first women to float through the entire Grand Canyon were Elzada Clover and Lois Jotter, passengers on pioneer river-runner Norm Nevills's first Grand Canyon commercial trip in 1938. Elzada, a botany professor, had met Nevills in Mexican Hat, Utah, when she was collecting specimens. Nevills, who had already run two tourist trips downriver through Glen Canyon to Lee's Ferry, asked Elzada if she would be interested in planning an expedition through the Grand Canyon to study botany. The next year, Nevills's three wooden boats headed toward Lee's Ferry, but apparently there were personality conflicts along the way. When they arrived at the Ferry, their trip began to disintegrate. Some historians believe that the trip continued only because of Elzada's determination to find replacements for the deserting boatmen.

When Buzz Holmstrom, an adventurer who had just traversed the Canyon solo the year before, heard of Nevills's intended trip carrying women passengers, he remarked, "Women have their place in this world, but they do not belong in the canyons of the Colorado."[1]

Well, he was a little mistaken. A few women have been in the Grand Canyon almost twenty years, and in November of 1990, more than two hundred people gathered at a river outfitter's warehouse to celebrate Georgie's eightieth birthday and fortieth year on the river. In the spring after her next birthday, Georgie would be gone, passing on to her next

1. David Lavender, *River Runners of the Grand Canyon*, p. 94.

adventure. But that night, her blue eyes shone like a teenage girl's as she danced at her birthday bash. One boatwoman said, "To be eighty years old in the Grand Canyon . . . you wouldn't think of your grandma running a boat in the Grand Canyon. Georgie doesn't care. That's her life. That's her happiness. As long as she's alive, she intends to partake in it—and there's a lot of people that love her for it."

Georgie said, "I was born under a lucky star." But, actually, in 1911, she was born into a poor, essentially fatherless, family in Chicago. Perhaps Georgie's mother was her lucky star. "My mother said, 'You can't get any lower because you're on the bottom, [but] you've got good health and spirit, so go for it!' " And Georgie did. After marrying at sixteen and giving birth to a daughter, Georgie and her husband set off for California on bicycles to find their fortune, "which was not a stunt; we didn't have any money." She loved Los Angeles and soon sent for the rest of her family. During the war years, she trained to ferry military planes within the States. In 1944, her daughter was killed in a bicycling accident, a tragedy Georgie may never have gotten over. But she did find renewal on the river.

Encouraged by friends, she attended a Sierra Club lecture by Harry Aleson, which led to the two of them swimming the Colorado. (Georgie was no stranger to cold water; she had grown up swimming in frigid Lake Michigan.) She and Harry hiked into the lower Grand Canyon with meager supplies and life jackets and jumped into the river. They tried to stay together by holding each other's wrists as they swam, or more literally, as they were tossed, spun, and submerged for four days by the muddy river, which was speeding along at 48,000 cubic feet per second (cfs). Georgie fell in love—with the Colorado. She and Harry came back into the lower Canyon the next year, this time bringing a small flimsy raft but nearly dying of thirst while hiking in. In the following years, she ran many Southwestern canyons, including Escalante, Cataract, Lodore, and Glen Canyon. Using the small military surplus rafts available after World War II, Georgie spent her vacations (from her Los Angeles real estate business) running share-the-expense vacations for friends and acquaintances. In 1952, she rowed through the entire Grand Canyon, with the exception of a few portages where she was helped by two boatmen who were now running Nevills's river company. Georgie had found her home and spent the rest of her life sharing it with others.

When she was running the high and wild Colorado back in 1954, she was frustrated with how frequently her small rafts flipped. Georgie had no fear of swimming and loved the big water. "I like rapids—always did and always will." But figuring that the idea of swimming rapids would not attract many passengers, she lashed three fourteen-foot rowing rafts together. These "triple rigs" were nicknamed *G-rigs* (for Georgie) and handled with sweep oars. Not only did this design make the boats more stable, it greatly increased the passenger-carrying capacity. Further, Georgie could save time by using a motor during the flat stretches. Using big boats and motors attracted more passengers, and began discussions about river-trip aesthetics that continue to this day.

In 1955, Georgie put together her giant G-rigs—three thirty-seven-foot, inflatable, military-surplus bridge pontoons tied together, creating a twenty-seven-foot-wide motorboat. Other early adventurers and outfitters had used various boat types: wooden boats and various-sized inflatable rafts propelled by either oars or motors. Georgie's new rig design, with some modifications, would be used by the majority of

Canyon river companies. Georgie said, "They'd call me crazy woman when I'd come into Temple Bar [take-out on Lake Mead]. I'd just laugh, have a beer, and go on because it didn't bother me any." Georgie could afford to "pay no attention"; she was her own boss, doing what she loved—an inspiration to all women who saw her on the water.

Fewer than two hundred people had floated through the Canyon when Georgie started running her G-rigs. Running rivers was considered a reckless thing to do, and only a few daring individuals attempted the roaring rapids of the Colorado. But soon, more and more people were discovering river running, the Grand Canyon, and perhaps the wilder side of themselves. In the 1960s, Americans were becoming aware of the wildland vacations available to them. Tourists signed on with outfitters like Georgie, who ran trips themselves or hired boatmen to assist with the essentials of running a river trip. Their job was to successfully navigate a boat from put-in to take-out, cook meals, talk about the ecology and history of the place, lead hikes, handle emergencies, and—most important—show people a good time.

Today, some river companies still are operated by or carry the names of some of these early outfitters: Hatch, Sanderson, and Ron Smith, to name a few. What began as a hobby eventually became a business. And for many river guides, what began as a summer job eventually became a career—albeit a seasonal career, May through September, with no retirement or health benefits.

In 1964, fifteen miles above the beginning of the Grand Canyon, the gates of Glen Canyon Dam closed, shutting off the natural muddy flow of the Colorado River. Spring floods of 120,000 cfs would be seen no more. The dam caused major ecological changes along the river, most visibly tamarisk growth, lack of driftwood, beach erosion, and clear water. The water flowing out from the deep artificial lake behind the dam was clear and cold, about fifty degrees. The dam helped catalyze a business boom because river runners could count on a fairly consistent flow between 3,000 to 29,000 cfs. The water would not drop out from under boats in the autumn or rise suddenly from unusual rain or spring runoff. (However, as we will see, there would be some unplanned events.)

Between 1965 and 1971, the number of people going down the river grew from 547 per year to 10,385. By 1972, almost 16,500 people had floated through the Canyon. The Grand Canyon National Park Service realized that, unless limits were set, overcrowding would destroy the pristine river corridor and the river experience. In 1973, the Park Service essentially froze the number of people allowed down the river, holding to the 1972 use level: 92 percent of the allotment was for commercial trips and the remaining 8 percent for noncommercial or private use. (Years later, due to public and business pressure, the private trip percentage and the total number of trips would increase.) The existing outfitters were given first preference for National Park commercial concessionaire status. After 1973, anyone who wanted to float through the Canyon had to apply either for a private permit (and probably wait years for a turn) or pay one of the licensed outfitters, or river companies, for a trip. If someone wanted to carry paying passengers, he or she had to work for one of the outfitters—not always an easy task if that someone happened to be a woman.

The women after Georgie were in a different world. By the early 1970s, the pioneer days of river exploration and creating river companies in the Grand Canyon were past. Georgie—a remarkable character with many adventures behind her—was in her early forties when she rowed the Canyon for the first time. The women who followed were in their twenties. The early seventies were also a time of transition, where women as well as men were changing their ideas of what constituted women's work.

There weren't nearly as many women as men asking to work as adventure guides; but a few who *were* asking heard some interesting responses. "You're a pretty girl, but we don't hire girls," said the manager of one river company to an eager applicant. That was in 1981—thirty years after Georgie started running her boats and almost four years after other Canyon boatwomen had begun leading river trips. The hiring of women guides continued to evolve unevenly, because each of the twenty river companies were like different countries with different traditions, crews, and leaders. Some of them, depending on their backgrounds and deeply ingrained ways of thinking, were more receptive than others to the idea of women running boats down the Colorado.

The companies run two different types of boats, oar-powered and motor-powered. A Canyon *oar raft* is fairly easy to envision—it is usually about eighteen feet long and looks like an oversized inflatable life raft with metal frames strapped on top for carrying gear. The guide sits near the center of the boat and rows with ten-foot-long wooden oars. Four to five rafts travel together, each carrying about four passengers. A small percentage of the boats rowed on the river are beautifully painted wooden *dories*—sleek, eighteen-foot boats equipped with storage hatches.

The big Grand Canyon motor rigs have various designs, but all are put together by strapping inflatable tubes to each other and tying a frame across the top. One design has twenty-two-foot cylindrical tubes attached to either side of a thirty-three-foot oblong donut tube. Other designs consist of four or five long cylindrical tubes tied side-by-side. The size of these large rigs varies depending on their design—thirty-three feet by twenty-seven feet, thirty-seven feet by eighteen feet, etc. All are capable of carrying sixteen people. Motor rigs travel either alone or in pairs, and are powered by twenty-five- or thirty-five-horsepower engines. A boatman, or pilot, stands in the rear and steers the boat with the three-foot extension handle attached to the motor. Some pilots have added the luxury of a chair for flatwater driving, and some, the comfort of earplugs. Both motor and oar boats carry all the gear necessary for the entire length of the trip. Motor trips generally take eight to nine days to travel through the Canyon. Oar trips are on the water for two weeks.

While eight of the twenty outfitters usually run oar trips, only one-fifth of the Canyon's commercial trips are oar trips because five of the six largest companies (the companies granted the most user days from the National Park) usually run motor rigs.

In the mid-1970s, three of the five women guiding boats for a full season worked for oar companies. By the end of the 1970s, almost all the oar companies and two of the motor companies had hired one full-time female guide. In addition to the eleven boatwomen profiled in this book, the following women guided commercial passengers in the 1970s.

In 1974, Barbara Thomas ran a *paddleboat* for ARTA's white-water school (a paddle guide shouts commands and rudders while the passengers paddle). Bebe Salazar, the food, equipment, and shuttle organizer at OARS, rowed her first boat downriver because a boatman canceled at the last minute. In the next few years, Bebe ran several more "last-minute" trips carrying discounted passengers before she ran a few trips carrying full-fare customers.

In 1976, Georgia Gloecker, after doing more than sixty motor trips with her husband, piloted her own rig for two seasons. That same year, Ote Dale convinced Clare Quist, owner of Moki Mac, to let her row three trips for him. (Previous to that, as an unpaid motorboat trainee for another company, Ote essentially ran a boatman's rig for nine trips.) Ote was followed at Moki Mac by Pam Quist (Clare's wife) and Millet Gray, who both worked for the next five years.

By 1977, Marylou Mowrer had started rowing for OARS. Joy Ungricht had rowed for Harris and continued doing occasional Canyon trips (as well as first ascents down many foreign rivers). Jessica Youle rowed trips for her company, AZRA. In 1978 and 1979, Kathy Howe rowed for Ken Sleight. As the decade drew to a close, Kimmie Johnson, Nancy Brian, and Ann Cassidy all had rowed boats down for OARS.

By the mid-1980s, all the oar companies and four more motor companies had hired female guides. When I began the research for this book in 1990, approximately 16 percent of the outfitters' core crews, or full-season guides, were women. Depending on the outfitter, the percentage of women working on core crews varies from 0 to 44 percent. There are considerably more women rowing than piloting motor rigs.

All the early Canyon boatwomen, through a combination of luck and desire, were able to set the groundwork for more women to work in the Canyon. "If we'd screwed up, history would have to be rewritten," said one boatwoman. "If we hadn't been able to handle the boats, do you think they would have put another one of us on? It would have been a long time. So we did it! And it was fun!"

It was, indeed, the best of times.

CHAPTER 2

The River Journey

To many river runners, floating into the Grand Canyon for the first time feels like coming home. But for some newcomers, it seems just the opposite. As one boatwoman describes it, "You truly walk through the door into a different reality. The place is such an assault on your senses—the massive cliffs, the strange plants, the shrill cicadas, the intense heat, and the swirling water. But you're held up because the intensity of everything buoys you up."

If you haven't been down there, let me give you a brief glimpse of the environment. If you have been there, let this help you travel back in your memory.

Lee's Ferry, Mile 0 on river maps, is where river runners have begun Grand Canyon trips ever since the gates of upstream Glen Canyon Dam closed. The high cliffs of the Grand Canyon fold down into the earth at Lee's Ferry, and rainbow-colored hills of soft shale allow us road access to the Colorado River. We won't have such access until 225 miles downstream.

The guides spend half a day rigging, sweating in the desert sun—unloading the truck, blowing up boats, assembling frames, stashing supplies into waterproof containers, and tying all the gear securely onto the boats. The next morning, our passengers arrive by chartered bus; after an introductory talk, we climb into our boats and pull out onto the river. Almost immediately, we are bobbing through a noisy riffle. We can see an abandoned dirt road from the old ferry working its way up through the small cliffs on the left bank. Then, Lee's Ferry disappears behind us as the river bends left and takes us into another small rapid. After that, the walls begin to climb and the river flows wide, flat and steady, at about four miles per hour. In a few miles, we float under Navajo Bridge, a shiny span of metal arching across the river. The cliff walls are starting to get considerably higher now; a semi-truck going across the bridge looks like a kid's toy.

Navajo Bridge is practically the last we will see of civilization as we know it.[1] As swallows dart overhead, our passengers study the cliffs, and some might wonder if they could climb out anywhere. Then, at Mile 8, we hear the rumble of upcoming Badger Rapid. We cannot actually see the rapid, only an approaching drop-off with white spray jumping behind it. As we drift closer, we see rocks and white waves spreading out before us. Then the boats slide down a slick tongue of water and drop into the roar. Waves build in front and to the side. We ride smoothly over the first, only to have the next crash over us. The passengers hold on tight as the boats buck and twist. Drenched and excited, our passengers begin to understand why we considered the white water below Lee's Ferry merely a riffle. The guides, dripping wet and grinning, remember again why they love this big river. We are all eager for the 160 rapids yet to come: for House Rock, the Roaring Twenties, Hance, the Gems. Three miles downstream, after

1. The next bit of civilization is eighty-eight miles downstream when we pass under the narrow suspension bridge that leads to Phantom Ranch, the destination of the famous Canyon mule ride.

Soap Creek Rapid, even the flat water begins to dance, as the Colorado glides and swirls along the sculptured, dark red sandstone walls jutting into the river. The rim looks to be a thousand feet away now; the sky narrows to a band of the clearest blue. There is no longer the option of leaving, and who would want to, as we are embraced by a world of rock and water.

Days pass, and the river carries us down deep into time—five hundred million years, two billion years—as the water carves through ever-older rock layers, exposing sediments deposited before dinosaurs walked the planet and, some say, before man. As we read the Canyon's geology, we are beginning to *feel* the reality of our ever-changing planet: mountains rose and eroded, seas advanced and receded. Our minds, unable to comprehend the billions of years we are seeing, take comfort in memorizing the names of the different rock layers: Kaibab Limestone, Tapeats Sandstone, Bright Angel Shale.

As the river currents twist and turn our boats, we watch these rock layers, each one over two hundred feet thick, climb higher and higher, each tier a different texture and color. Sheer and broken cliffs are painted in vibrant salmons, reds, buffs, and browns. Slopes and plateaus, painted in greens, mauves, and maroons, alternate between the vertical cliff faces. Their surfaces are littered with talus and house-sized boulders broken off from the cliffs above. Cacti, shrubs, and tufts of grass grow where they can.

Each bend in the river, each corridor, offers new wonders. Our boats glide past geometrically chiseled cliffs, colored deep salmon and shadowed with a black stain called desert varnish. We drift between massive red limestone walls rising straight out of the river, smooth as marble and riddled with caves. Caves containing two- to four-thousand-year-old relics from ancestors whose stories we have forgotten. Water seeps stain high alcoves. A stream bursts out from a wall, and jewels of water tumble down fern- and flower-lined rock. We float past thin-bedded, gray cliffs scalloped with edges sharp as knives. We drift past ancient lava flows that, millions of years ago, spilled over the canyon rim. We float alongside brown, grainy sandstone cliffs, layered like pancakes, honeycombed with overhangs large enough to shelter us during a thunderstorm or just big enough to shade a rattlesnake from the midday sun. White sand beaches stretch out along the river, lined with slender arrow-weed and feathered tamarisk trees. River-worn boulders in varied hues gather along beaches and deltas. Side canyons open to the river, beckoning us to explore them.

Hundreds of canyons, narrow and wide, named and unnamed. Short dead-end canyons choked with boulders. Long canyons that promise routes to the rim. Canyons alive with the sound of frogs and running water. Dry canyons with thirsty shrubs rattling in the wind. Canyons we stroll up, hopping over boulders and studying gleaming pools with childish joy. Canyons we struggle up, half delirious from the vibrating heat.

During the hot monsoon season, side canyons can suddenly flash-flood and flow red. Dark clouds, sudden wind, and thunder rolling down the Canyon announce the coming storm. Lightning cracks across the sky; sheets of rain or hail slam into us, and wind controls the boats. As the storm builds, we may see red muddy waterfalls gush over the walls, and hear rocks, loosened from the downpour, crash down from the cliffs. Humbled and exalted, we howl into the storm. After the short violent outburst, the wind switches, clouds clear, and cliffs sparkle. The air is pungent with the smell of satisfied desert plants and moist earth.

The whole tapestry of desert life begins to unveil itself: A hawk flies high along the cliff, alert for any movement. The heart-shaped leaves of a bright green redbud tree cast quivering shadows against a slab of rock. A mesquite root tenaciously pries apart a boulder. Lizards sun themselves on warm rocks. Red ants swarm a fallen beetle. A metallic, blue-black wasp drags a tarantula across a dry creek bed. A muscular bighorn ram climbs a cliff and looks back, his full-curled horns silhouetted against the sky. A canyon wren calls out her song. When the sun falls below the rim and the canyon cools, desert night life begins. Bats take to the air, mice scurry out from their shelters, beetles crawl over sand dunes, scorpions hunt, and the striped gray tail of a ring-tailed cat moves like a ghost over boulders.

Deep within the Canyon, seventy-seven miles downriver, we enter into the dark bottom of the world—the Inner Gorge, more than a vertical mile below the rim. For almost forty miles, we swirl between hard, shiny black walls a thousand feet high—two-billion-year-old rock we call Vishnu Schist and Brahma Schist. These ancient cliffs are folded, cracked, fluted, polished. Veins of pink granite slither through the walls. Although the river flows fast through here, there is no easily perceivable downstream current, only endless eddies swirling and boiling up against each other.[2]

In the Inner Gorge, our reverie of gazing at the Canyon is often interrupted by the sound of a low roar rumbling downstream, because between these black walls are some of the most legendary and exhilarating rapids in the Grand Canyon:

2. Eddies are created when the downstream current is deflected by projections or midstream rocks. Water, ever adapting its form to terrain, flows back upstream—in a sense, to fill in what it missed.

Sockdolager, Grapevine, Horn Creek, Granite, and Hermit. Noisy, roaring water that dances between the canyon walls. Rapids with waves higher than our boats are long. Smooth, undulating waves that entice us to ride them. Pulsating, crashing waves that engulf our boats, filling them to the brim. Folding waves that stall our boats momentarily, bending the tubes back. Roller-coaster waves that we climb and free-fall down. And then there is Crystal Rapid: the worry, the fear, and the sweet adrenaline high of running this awesome spectacle of white water—it is a powerful display of water building into crashing waves, tumbling over barely submerged rocks, and surging and boiling along the cliff.

The river is a heart-stopping fifty degrees, and emerald green, except when the side canyons flash-flood and run red. Then the Colorado reverts to its pre-dam earth color—red-brown, thick mudwater. Mudwater does not splash; it slaps, it convulses, lifts, and falls. It slithers over rocks, foams in eddies, and builds into sculptured waves—waves that crash over the boat, weighing more than water should, and leaving us pounded, covered in mud, and grinning happy.

After we make camp and as the sun sets, we watch the river glow tangerine orange, coral, and blue, reflecting colors high above. Distant cliffs catch fire and burn scarlet and bright orange against the sky. As the light fades, the river keeps on flowing past the hard, dark rock—teasing it, licking it, mocking its solemn solidarity and taking it down, down to the sea.

For two weeks, we river travelers are both awed and comforted by the immensity of the Grand Canyon. We are alternately wet and dry, delighted and scared, silly and reverent, social and solitary. Intense heat slows us down; cold water revives us. Our concerns simplify. We take time to notice small details: the veins on a dragonfly's wings, the feel of a smooth river-worn stone. At night, as the river softly murmurs, we gaze out into the heavens. Something inside us responds. We remember forgotten feelings. We have revelations.

And we have fun.

Occasionally, we catch glimpses of the Canyon rim. But as time passes, the world beyond the rim becomes more and more unreal. No longer strangers, we have become a tribe that has always lived with the flow of the river. Even our first days on the river seem like distant memories. We have become totally immersed in the Grand Canyon.

Until take-out.

At Diamond Creek, a side canyon at Mile 226, we leave the river, driving our boats and passengers up a graded, sometimes just recently flooded, dirt road. Some trips bypass this first possible take-out, and float through Lower Granite Gorge on out to Lake Mead, the artificial lake made by Hoover Dam. About twelve miles past Diamond Creek, what was once the mighty Colorado slows down, backed up by the lake. At Mile 276, this river/lake flows out between the Grand Wash Cliffs, and the Grand Canyon abruptly ends.

River trips also end abruptly, and members of the tribe are left to make their own adjustments—to leaving each other, to leaving the Grand Canyon. For the river guides in love with the Canyon, it makes perfect sense to drive back to the beginning and start over. The basic ingredients of the next trip will be the same, but the people, the light, the water, and the Canyon are ever changing.

CHAPTER 3

Louise Teal

Marilyn Sayre

In her home in the east San Francisco Bay area, on a kitchen wall next to a refrigerator plastered with shopping lists and children's drawings held up by plastic alphabet magnets, Marilyn Sayre has hung a plaque. The plaque is actually an old piece of driftwood hanging by a worn-out piece of cord. The black magic marker writing on it is faded but still legible:

THE GREAT RACE

Ms. Marilyn beats five men. Colorado River, 1976

In 1973, three years before that obscure rowing race, Marilyn Sayre became the first woman since Georgie to run a commercial boat through the Grand Canyon. Marilyn is a striking and capable, slim six-foot blonde. Her light brown eyes are straightforward and analytical, except when they are crinkled up in laughter.

Her first trip through the Canyon in 1970 was on a large motorboat as a tourist with the American River Touring Association (ARTA) company. "I was twenty-four years old and doing computer engineering programming for General Electric. My carpool partner had signed up for a motor trip through the Grand Canyon. At the last minute, his buddy decided not to go with him, so he asked me if I wanted to come. I said, 'Sure!'

"I had no idea what I was getting into. I knew nothing about the Grand Canyon, absolutely nothing. I'd been hiking in the Sierras, I'd been kayaking rivers in California, but that was always just running down the river, never an overnight trip. Nothing like being in the Grand Canyon and hiking up all those side canyons—day after day after day, in the wilderness with nothing to interrupt it. It was one of those experiences where I never wanted to go back home.

"And then halfway down the trip I met Allen Wilson, a boatman who hiked in to join our trip. It was love at first sight. Well, maybe after a couple of days," Marilyn added, giggling. "Allen laughed at everything and everybody loved him. We spent the rest of the trip hanging out together. I particularly remember going down into Deer Creek narrows, jumping into the stream, and crawling down all these amazing waterfalls.

"He came to visit a couple of times in the Bay Area and we wrote each other all the time. He wanted me to come down to Arizona and be with him, but it was a major decision in my life to do something so radical. But I did it. I quit my job."

She wrote ARTA's owner and was told that she could work as Allen's assistant, or swamper, a common slot for girlfriends who wanted to be on the river.

"I had no thoughts of having my own boat, but I was hankering to drive those darn things. See, this has always been me. I go into something figuring I can't do it, but I have this little itch in me that wants to do it. I want to try everything. Allen started teaching me about running the engine. Actually, I had run motorboats when I was a kid because our family used to go waterskiing. I had two brothers, but I was the most adventuresome."

And what an adventure it was to drive thirty-three-foot motor rigs, especially through rapids when the river was low and technical—when rocks were exposed and the holes and pour-overs (sharp drops over submerged rocks) felt like small waterfalls. Even at six feet, Marilyn had to "peek over the load to see the rapids. There were all these duffel bags and people piled in front of me." As the waves crashed over her and the boat pitched and rocked, Marilyn stood in the back, in the motor well, with one hand on the motor's extension handle maneuvering the rig. She could not over-rev in waves, or water would be sucked into the carburetor, and the motor would die. And she had to protect the prop from crunching on rocks. If a rock was deep enough, she could just raise her motor but still keep the prop slightly in the water by lifting the nearby jackass handle—a long handle that would leverage the motor up. But if the rock was close to the surface, she had to turn around, reach over the back of the motor, and tilt it completely out of the water.

"I just yanked the whole motor up, then held onto another part of the boat with one hand and the motor with the other hand, set my feet squarely on the bottom of that motor well, and just hung on for dear life.

"There were times the motor would die. I have vague memories of floating up to the lip of a rapid and trying to start the engine like mad, but I don't think that happened on any major rapids where I really needed that motor. And those big boats got you through most everything. I mean, to tip one of those things over takes a lot.

"The whole thing came pretty agreeably to me. Running a motor rig downriver was like driving a car down a moving street."

Allen said Marilyn had learned how to run a boat quicker

than anyone he had ever trained. He also recalled quite a few times when Marilyn was ignored by other boatmen. For instance, on one take-out, Allen had to hike up the dirt road to find out what had happened to the truck, leaving Marilyn and two other boatmen to de-rig two boats. When he got back, he found the other boatmen, their boat completely de-rigged, hanging out in the shade drinking a beer while Marilyn was still out de-rigging Allen's boat. "Those darn guys hadn't lifted a finger to help her."

On another take-out, Marilyn received some surprising news. "I think it was after my third trip; Mike the manager met us and said, 'Marilyn, in two more trips you're going to get your own boat.'

"I just about croaked. There were butterflies in my stomach just zooming around. I had never even considered having my own boat, I just thought I'd kind of do this with Allen—not me in my own boat with all those people by myself! Maybe Mike had asked Allen how I was doing or heard from other boatmen, I don't know. And I hadn't run all of the major rapids. I hadn't run Crystal yet."

Crystal Rapid lies at Mile 98, where the river roars between imposing, twisted black cliffs deep within the Inner Gorge. With rare exception, all Grand Canyon rapids are caused by side canyons depositing boulders in the river. Crystal was born December 1966 after fourteen inches of rain fell in thirty-six hours. A thousand-year flood, or more precisely, a debris flow—a three-story wall of muddy water and boulders—roared down Crystal Creek, dumping tons of boulders into the Colorado. Prior to the dam's construction, the river's powerful spring floods would have carved a reasonable route through such obstacles to the Colorado's seaward flow. After the dam was built, as when Crystal's debris flow occurred, this minor rapid transformed into a permanent major rapid. In the new Crystal, a long, smooth, V-shaped entry ("tongue") of the rapid sped down into a twenty-foot exploding wave capable of flipping boats.

Most unplanned swims through Grand Canyon rapids are fairly safe if you are wearing a life jacket, except for the danger of hypothermia from the fifty-degree water. But right below Crystal's big waves is the Rock Island, a sieve of mid-stream boulders that threatens unwilling swimmers with a potentially battering swim through rocks and pour-overs.

Marilyn said, "If you screwed up there, it seemed that the people would swim forever. They'd come out of the water cold as icicles. It was such a hard rapid to keep control in because there were so many rocks on that right-hand edge—they'd just bump us into that big hole. [Big waves are often called holes.] I didn't want to hit those rocks with a motor because I'd shear a pin and then I'd be useless—I'd have no power after that. I wanted to keep my motor in the deepest part of the water away from the rocks, but I didn't mind my front end bumping against rocks as long as it didn't throw my boat out of control.

"So I hugged the right-hand shore, faced the boat to the right, watched the hole coming down on my left, and tried to go by.

"Well, the first time I ran it, Allen was standing in the back of the boat with me. We hit a rock with the front of the boat. I mean a big rock. It completely threw the boat to the left and so we were heading toward the hole—sideways. Allen was yelling at me, 'Straighten out the boat! *Straighten out the boat!*' So I straightened out the boat. I gunned that engine as hard as I could and straightened out the boat. That boat went into that hole and came up on end. The whole rig stayed vertical for a few seconds and shuddered. We were literally hanging by our nails. I thought the boat was going to flip. Allen thought the boat was going to flip. But it didn't flip.

"I was so scared, and that night Allen said—and he had never talked like this to me before—'Don't ever do that again.' And I told him, 'I don't want my own boat; I don't want to do this.' But he said, 'It'll be all right. You're going to be fine. Just don't do that again.' "

And she was fine. In fact, more than fine; Marilyn was always considered extremely competent by her peers. That first season, Marilyn realized she was the only woman besides Georgie running her own boat. "That made me feel nice, but it was the luck of the draw. And it was also luck . . . well no, actually, it was not good luck that most companies felt like women couldn't do anything. ARTA was just beginning to feel that women could work. Only a few years before that, Allen was considered too small to work on the Colorado River. And he was very strong—wiry, but strong."

One summer, they both tried to work on the upper Colorado in Utah. Although outfitters were willing to give Allen a boat, they would not let Marilyn run her own rig.

Marilyn and Allen ran Grand Canyon motor trips for the next two years. I remember the first time I saw Marilyn's bright, toothpaste-ad smile shining across the river—probably grinning at me because she had a boatload of Green Berets.

"They were training for some secret expedition somewhere. They wouldn't tell us which river, who knows, Africa or South America, but they needed to learn to run rivers so they decided to practice in the Grand Canyon. They couldn't deal with me running the boat at all. They didn't get it. The only guys that would talk to me were the captains. I think women were just a part of gambling, cigarettes, and booze to the rest of them. I remember a few remarking that they'd rather be in Las Vegas gambling than sitting on 'this stupid boat.' But it was great at camp—the captains would tell the privates to set up camp, get dinner started and they would—hup, hup—do it all. Allen and I would just sit around."

Marilyn learned to row by helping Allen run a few off-season trips for the U.S. Geological Survey. "We learned a lot about geology because the geologists would just gab away about the rocks. In fact, the joke was that they'd head up some hillside and stop to talk about rocks every twenty feet because they were so out of breath. Of course, we were about twenty years younger than all those poor guys."

By 1975, Marilyn started rowing ARTA's snout rigs. Snouts were rather unique twenty-two-foot, one-ton boats, equipped with thirteen-foot oars—big oar boats designed for big water. Snouts had to be positioned in the right place when entering a rapid because there was no correcting them later. Those boats would just keep on tracking in the direction they were pointed. Snout rowers learned to use the current as much as possible, making every move count because no one could pull those thirteen-foot oars all day and have any energy left for hikes or making camp. These practically unpivotable beasts were created by setting a four-foot-wide steel-and-wood frame between two inflated military surplus pontoons. This design provided more than enough room for six passengers and all the necessary downriver gear. The final touch to these sleek scows was a few wooden crates of fruit piled on the back. It was considered somewhat of a miracle that anyone, much less a woman, could row these rigs.

Marilyn could row quite well—plus she enjoyed a little competition. "On some trips, we took along a little paddleboat that we'd pull out once in awhile, usually in the calmer stretches. One day five men were paddling in it beside my boat. We just kept going a little faster. Those guys paddled a little harder, and I started rowing a little harder, and pretty soon we were going full steam down the river. My arms were just killing me, I was rowing so hard. But I finally beat them. Those guys were so impressed that they gave me an award that night—a driftwood plaque commemorating the Great Race of 1976. I still have it. It's hanging on the wall in my kitchen."

Marilyn always enjoyed showing people how to row and read the water. "Maybe more passengers were willing to try it when they saw a woman running the boats," she said. "That may have encouraged people more for some of the wrong reasons, but it worked out well.

"I'd try to encourage women, but very few would try. A few men were willing. I mean, if just your lowly woman could row, well, hell, it's got to be easy. It was such a riot because the men would get on those heavy snout oars, and I'd explain to them how to do it, and you'd see looks on their faces like, oh, this is a cinch. And pretty soon, all the other boats were downstream, and my new rower would be panting somewhere on the wrong side of the river lost in a giant eddy going round and round."

Marilyn worked in the Canyon for about four years, running twenty-five trips. After she and Allen broke up, she did not enjoy running river trips as much. "It was a thing we'd done together," she said. That, and Marilyn did not feel like she got along well with some of the boatmen. For one thing, a few of them partied too much for her taste. "Some of the guys were just great, and others . . . there was this undercurrent. I mean, I saw myself as an equal, but I felt, although they never said anything overtly, that some of them did not want me there, that they would rather have another guy. It was the first time in my whole life that I ever really experienced what I'd call male chauvinism. I was young and idealistic, and it really put me out. I became even more aware of it when I wasn't with Allen. Maybe I was a threat to them because I wanted to be involved in more of the decisions. I don't know; I never figured it out. I couldn't warm up to them, and they couldn't warm up to me. It made it hard for me to work down there."

Marilyn was also beginning to feel pressured by the responsibility and, paradoxically, was getting cocky. "I felt like nothing was going to happen to me, but then I realized that my attitude was going to make something happen. And then there was an incident in Deubendorff Rapid when the water was really low.

"I didn't make a bad run. There was this one-armed man on the trip, and I had him sitting in a part of the boat I thought was safe. But we were banging around so much that he dislocated his shoulder. A doctor on the trip popped it back in, and he was okay. He was a tough old bird, but even though it was [just] bad luck, I felt very bad.

"And then another trip blew me away. We came upon a motorboat that had gone into . . . what's the name of that huge rock you have to go to the right of? Yeah, Bedrock. We came down about fifteen minutes after a motor trip had flipped a thirty-three-footer there. There were people and equipment everywhere. Nobody was hurt badly, but I remember looking into the eyes of the people who were sitting on the rocks. They looked shell-shocked, they were so scared."

A couple of other things affected Marilyn's decision to quit. "I was real sick of the money—what was it, $35 or $40 a day? And it was starting to get old a little bit in the sense that people were a big part of your life for twelve days, and then they were gone. You might see them once at a reunion, maybe, or they might write you once a year. It was really hard to get close, have them go, and then have another group come in. I felt like I was a tour guide putting on a show, and that was very exhausting, very tiring. I got burned out."

But before Marilyn quit, she and I ran a few trips together. I had started rowing snout rigs the year after Marilyn ran her own motor rig. The same year, the owner of ARTA sold his Grand Canyon operation to his son Robert Elliott and Robert's wife, Jessica Youle. They renamed it Arizona Raft Adventures (AZRA). Today, no one at AZRA is particularly concerned if more women than men are on a trip's crew, but in the mid-seventies it was different. Even though Rob and Jessie practically pioneered hiring boatwomen in the Canyon, they were worried about how passengers would react to women guides. When Marilyn and I were scheduled to row together on the same trip, it was considered a big step, sort of a risky experiment. Before that, we would only see each other on the river if our trips happened to pass. In fact, that's how the AZRA nickname "hag" started. Whenever we would pass each other on the river, I would yell, "Hey, you old bat!" and she would yell back, "What's happening, you old hag!" Whoever thought that two decades later many AZRA boatwomen would still enjoy calling each other "hags."

On the hill above Crystal one day, I realized that Marilyn would soon be leaving the river. We were scouting for the best route through the rapid when she said to me, "You know what I've been thinking?"

"What?" I asked, anxious for any advice that would help me run my boat.

"Louise, I just can't figure out whether to make kitchen curtains or to buy them."

Incredible. Marilyn had already left the Canyon. She was gone.

Shortly thereafter, Marilyn moved back to the San Francisco Bay area and returned to computer programming. For three years, she rowed shells with a competitive crew team. "The scenery obviously couldn't hold a candle to the Grand Canyon, but it was my replacement activity—it was water, it was a boat. That tided me over."

Eventually, she fell in love with another programmer and changed her last name to Kremen. A few years later, she took on a job far more challenging than running Crystal: she started a family. Her subsequent years were rich with family and professional activities—including driving her three children around, keeping up a house, staying fit, and re-entering the business world by buying, renovating, and selling homes.

The last time I visited Marilyn in her tasteful neighborhood, she immediately took me upstairs to see all the slimy creatures her boys had collected: "You're the one friend who'd want to see these snakes, lizards, and toads." Then we drank tea and laughed about old times—about rowing those snouts, about places we had been. Marilyn reminisced about Havasu Creek, the musical turquoise stream that flows through a red-cliffed side canyon. Curved travertine dams create deep swimming holes, bubbling jacuzzis, and large and small waterfalls. There are pink rocks to crawl over, limestone cliffs perfect for jumping into deep pools, and polished white boulders just right for warming up after a swim. A soft sandy path winding through grapevines leads up to the next swimming hole, and farther on to hundred-foot waterfalls. Cottonwood and ash trees lining the creek provide shade from the heat. Anywhere, Havasu Canyon would be considered beautiful. In the desert, it seems unbelievable. Marilyn said, "I remember taking the people up there, getting practically naked, and jumping in all the pools. I mean, it was always a total day of ecstasy.

"You know, I learned so much down there from all the different roles I played as a guide. And that feeling that I could physically run those oar trips, that feeling of being strong and capable—that's something that's carried me through my life."

I asked her, "Do you ever miss being down there, Bat?"

"Oh, I've missed it terribly. I do miss running those rapids. I'd give my right arm to go down there again. I want to take my husband and kids down.

"The image I have most often is of lying down on top of my sleeping bag on warm nights. I'd be tired from the day, and I'd look up at the night sky and think—oh, I want to look at these stars for awhile; they're so beautiful. But I'd always fall asleep. The next thing I knew, some boatman was clanking around in the kitchen and I had to get up, and I'd missed those stars again."

We jabbered until it was time for her to pick up her kids. As she was getting ready to drive off, she said, "You know what you taught me?"

"What?" I asked, wondering what pearl of wisdom had guided her through the years since she had left the river.

"It was on that trip we did that first year. You showed me that when you have long hair, you don't start at the top to comb the tangles out. You start at the bottom.

"I teach that to my daughter now," she said, and gave me that big, toothpaste-ad grin as she pulled out of her driveway.

CHAPTER 4

David Edwards. Color slide.

Liz Hymans

"You've got crumbs on your cheek."

That is the first thing Liz Hymans said when we sat down for our official interview. She is not the type to sit there and wonder whether to mention the food all over your face. She will tell you.

With her deep throaty voice, dusky-haired Liz comes on direct, definite, and to the point—almost brusque. You might be put off by her manner if you did not notice her warm, laughing hazel eyes or if you had not heard other boatwomen credit Liz with giving them constant support when they first started, which was not always the case between woman guides. As one lady put it, "There was that coveted woman's slot and sometimes it was jealously guarded."

Liz's directness may have helped or hindered her. But the fact is, she was the first woman to be hired by a Grand Canyon outfitter on her own, without the backing of a mate. She was determined and not deterred by the word "no." As a frustrated fellow guide once told her, "Liz, you don't listen very well. But, I guess, if you listened you wouldn't be here."

Liz did not come from a rich family, and she figured out early on that "if you couldn't afford to do something as the leisure class, then you worked and got paid to do it." That is how she skied when she was growing up in Colorado, by teaching skiing. "I taught all over the place. I was in Winter Park for five seasons. I went to Norway for a year. I taught in Aspen and Telluride. I led a few college courses in cross-country skiing and winter survival. But then I needed something to do in the summer."

Liz discovered playing on melted water after a friend of hers picked up a hitchhiking boatman. The boatman's Utah river company was just starting up, running Cataract Canyon above Glen Canyon Dam, and they needed to put together a brochure. Liz's friend just happened to be a photographer and quickly volunteered to come on a river trip to take brochure pictures. On the trip, he was allowed to take a few friends along. Liz, one of those friends, remembers, "It was fifty bucks for five days. I noticed the boatman got to run the rapids and I didn't. And he got paid and I didn't. I thought—something's wrong with this picture. I asked how I could become a boatman. He said, 'You have to know someone.' And I said, 'Well, I don't know anybody, now what?' He suggested I go down to Lee's Ferry and try to get on as a swamper."

At that time, Lee's Ferry consisted of a few trailers for rent, a small restaurant, and the remains of Mormon settler John D. Lee's old stone buildings. The dirt ramp sloping down to the river was usually filled with rubber boats and frames in various stages of assembly. The boatmen, rigging in hundred-degree temperatures, looked forward to late afternoon when the upstream cliffs reflected a setting sun.

"So I went to Lee's Ferry on May 26, 1972. [She remembers most dates exactly.] People showed up with their rigs and I walked up and said, 'Hi! Do you need a swamper?' and they kind of looked me up and down and said, 'No, thanks.'

"After about four of those, I figured I needed a new approach, so I walked up and said, 'Can I help you load your boat?' Then they got a free sample of my work." She was rejected a lot, but she learned about the game and what companies were likely to take on a twenty-two-year-old woman.

Four days after she came to the Ferry, Pat and Dennis Prescott said she could come downriver with them. They had all been sitting around after rigging, passing wine and playing guitar. They said that if Liz would play guitar on demand plus give Dennis three guitar lessons, she could go on the trip. "So here it is, eighteen years later, and I still owe Dennis two guitar lessons," she chuckled.

Liz managed to get on a few more motor trips, and between stints on the ramp helping with rigging, she went around to the outfitters' offices that were within a half-day's drive of Lee's Ferry. "I ran into things like, 'Well, what's a nice little girl like you doing down here?' or stuff like, 'Why do you have to be a boatman? Couldn't you just marry one?' Basically, these were good, solid Mormon people who hated to see a girl out doing such rough work when it really wasn't necessary."

She persevered, hung out at the Ferry, helped load trips, and helped unload the "dailies" (fifteen-mile trips upriver to the dam). "They gave me leftover shrimp salad and all the lemonade I could drink." When it got too hot, she hung out in the culvert under Lee's Ferry Road.

In July, her permanent ticket down the Colorado drove in—outfitter George Wendt, owner of OARS' rowing trips. Turned out Liz knew one of his guides, Skip Horner. They had done a cross-country ski trip together over Red Table Mountain. "It was supposed to be a comfortable thirty-mile, two-day trip with a cabin to sleep in. But it turned into an epic fifty-five miles over rugged terrain and a bivouac, sleeping on our skis in a snowfield. The most wonderful part was the beauty of the surrounding high wilderness, especially by moon and starlight as we skied late into both nights. Skip got frostbitten toes. At the halfway point, he and three others took a steep eight-mile shortcut to the road. Three of us made it all the way, so Skip thought I could do anything after that, which helped."

And it helped that the boss, the person who actually did the hiring, was there. "To this day, George Wendt remembers first meeting me. He was sitting there packing food, and the next thing he knew, he was kind of shouldered out of the way, and there I was showing him I could work.

"We worked till midnight. I asked if he had any openings. 'No, not on this river.' So I said, 'Well, what about other rivers?' He said, 'Talk to me in the morning.'

"The next morning I asked him again. Well, he had an opening on a training trip in California, but he didn't want to say yes because then I'd go out there and expect to work, and he couldn't offer me any work. He really couldn't. So I said, 'Well, that's no problem, I could just get trained and work for someone else afterwards. I wouldn't bother you.' And he said, 'Well, give me a call.' I said, 'Okay, what's your number?' After four long-distance calls, he finally said yes. George has a real hard time saying no to people, and I don't like to listen to no, so we were a pretty good combination."

So Liz, like many guides, learned to row on a nine-mile stretch of the Stanislaus River, a clear rocky river in the Sierras that was soon to be dammed. The OARS warehouse was fairly typical of that stage of commercial river-running history—"an eight-by-ten storage shed in some farmer's backyard," according to Liz. Getting time rowing still did not come easy, but between doing shuttles and helping out any way she could, Liz wangled her way onto the river. At that time, she was the only woman rowing for OARS. "My first training trip was sitting in the boat watching another boatman row. I was a little frustrated, but I could see that I really wasn't in a position to squawk."

Downstream from Parrott's Ferry, the usual commercial Stanislaus take-out, was an easy stretch of river. When Liz went to meet one trip at Parrott's Ferry that was continuing on downriver, she came up with a plan to row her own boat. "Jamie was taking his boat out there, so I said, 'Listen, wouldn't it be easier if Jamie got in the truck and bought some beer (that's using the magic word), and I rowed his boat down, and then we can just take all of the boats out together?' Otherwise everybody would have to stop, carry the boat out, dry it out, roll it up, and put it in the truck because it was more than one person's worth of work with those old heavy things. So they thought, well, . . . yeah. I could see that they were real nervous about me rowing down, but never mind. I got in the boat, and I rowed the boat down to the end, and Jamie met us in the truck. So I did the lower half."

The next day Liz rowed on a training trip on the upper Stanislaus and then trained a boatman on the lower run. "You can imagine how much he learned from me," she chuckled. By the end of the summer, when a lot of George's main guides left to run his Grand Canyon trips, she was pretty much running the show—leading the two-day trips, hiring shuttle drivers, and buying the food. She asked George if she could go on the last Grand Canyon training trip, but there was no spot unless she wanted to ride with a guy named Bruce Keplinger. "The idea of *ride* with him didn't sound particularly appealing, but I figured—well, I've always believed that good luck happens to people who are ready for it, so I'll just go over there and get ready."

Liz worked off the OARS training fee by building boat frames for the trip. "It wasn't like today where you can call up and give your credit-card number and buy river equipment through catalogs. First, we went to George's mother's house to build frames in the driveway—sawed two-by-sixes, drilled holes for bolts, and countersank them. Then we went down to the junior high metal shop and sawed up steel bars for the thole pins (posts on the rowing frame that oars clip onto). Then we went off to the welding shop."

When all the equipment and boatmen arrived at the Ferry, luck was indeed waiting for Liz. Bruce Kleplinger looked her up and down and said, "Well, I've rowed it; you row it." So she did, except for maybe four major rapids. Liz said, "That was September 12th through the 27th, as I recall. I ended that summer with a hundred dollars in my pocket, after I'd paid for my training trips—ten dollars apiece, and the Grand Canyon training fee was one hundred dollars in those days." The next year she worked in California and did one more Canyon training trip. After that, Liz worked from two to ten trips in the Canyon per season. She figures she has racked up over ninety trips by now.

Working in the Canyon does not mean just rowing boats. One of the best parts of the job is taking people up side canyons to places like Elves Chasm, Deer Creek, Stone Creek, Matkatamiba—magical places where the canyon wren's song beckons hikers up to delicate waterfalls bordered with maidenhair ferns and red monkey flowers. Well, actually, it is not just the bird's song beckoning, it is usually the guides urging people up the trails. The trails are not always trails, but routes over ledges and boulders, old Indian and bighorn sheep routes. And sometimes passengers are not looking at the scenery; they are watching their feet trying to avoid glancing down into a gaping void below them.

It took Liz a little time to get used to the hikes. "I had one of those watch-out mamas who was always saying, 'Don't go too close to the edge.' So I'd get on these hikes up Elves Chasm or Deer Creek where that little ledge is, and I'd be absolutely petrified. And I thought, there's no way I'm doing this. But then I thought, if I want to be the guide, I not only can't ask for help, I need to look like a guide. So, shit, exude confidence. What I'd do is turn around to the person behind me and say, 'Here, it's real easy, let me help you.' I'd put their feet and hands in the right places and tell them what to do, and the next person would haul them up. Then, after I jacked about three or four up ahead of me, I'd follow; [I'd] run ahead to the next tough spot and I'd go, 'No, really, it's not as hard as it looks, let me help you.'

"In those days, nobody admitted to fear. You couldn't. Boatmen seemed to thrive on an atmosphere of competition, and I was more looking for things like encouragement and support. It just wasn't that kind of business at all, so you had to look like you were made of steel the whole time.

"I remember the first time I saw Clavey Falls on the Tuolumne River [California]. We were paddling a small boat down on our days off and stopped to scout the rapid. The guys just looked at Clavey and said, 'Okay, let's go.' The boatmen had on their life jackets, but I sort of thought the life jackets should come off so we could portage (or carry the boats around) the rapid, because you obviously couldn't run it," Liz said, getting a chuckle in her deep voice.

"But I just did what they did. I buckled my life jacket and off we went. That was my first swim. The paddle commands were as follows: 'Hard forward! Back paddle! Ooooh, shit!' "

Quite a few years later, when Liz was leading a trip after the high water of 1983, she considered portaging again. As the crew members stood at Crystal Rapid, they could hear rocks rolling out in the river and practically feel the ground shake from the waves crashing. "I looked at it and thought, okay, let's say we walked the passengers, and we pulled as hard as we could . . . it still looked like a sixty percent chance of flipping. So out of five boats, that put three over and two chasing and everybody on shore going, 'Gee, did you see *that*?' The same sort of material was kind of going through the other guides' heads.

"To that point in our experience, basically, we had decided how to run—how many boats to send first, whether to walk the passengers—but we never really decided whether to run the rapid. It had never really been a question.

"Now, when I don't know what to do, I think, if I do that, how would that feel? So I was thinking, how would it feel to portage, and immediately, it felt great. I talked to the other guides in decreasing order of suspected agreement. It wasn't a problem; we all felt real good about portaging. It took half a day. Our decision was reinforced as we heard what went on in Crystal during that week."

Liz chuckled and said, "Two trips back, I ran both the big waves beginning in Crystal. I got in there, and my pull didn't feel quite right—I was surfing." The boat stalled on the upstream side of the first wave for a few seconds. "I went over the shoulder of the first wave spinning, so I tried to complete the spin, but I hadn't quite completed it when the second wave popped on me. I went tumbling out of the seat towards the low side of the boat. My hat fell in the river, and my oar somehow got pushed by the water so that it hit my neck and started pushing me back up on my feet. And I thought to myself—just a minute, I want my hat. That's my new hat. And I leaned over again to try and get my hat, but the oar hit me in the neck again as if to say, 'No, you *row*.' And I thought, so okay, the hat's a small price to pay. I'll row, I'll row. So I got back on my sticks and ran left of the Island."

When Liz first started her river job, a few things were less than perfect for her. "Some of the guys were a little difficult to be around at times. They liked to drink beer and smoke a lot, which both bore me. Then there was a lot of sexism. I can remember those guys sitting there making remarks about women walking by. Finally, one day some girl walked by, and I thought to myself, gosh, look at the breasts on that one. Then I thought, just a minute, there's something wrong with this, so I decided to fight fire with fire. The next time a couple walked by and one of the guys said something along the lines of, 'Oh, what an ass, I think I'm in love,' I said, 'Well, nice-looking guy, but nah, it doesn't look like he has much in his pants.'

"For about two years I didn't hear any more comments like that. It was just wonderful."

Even after she had been rowing for some time, she felt that a few of the boatmen still acted condescendingly. "One guy was always pulling me aside at rapids and telling me what to do in front of the passengers. I thought that didn't really inspire confidence, so finally I said, 'Why are you telling me this stuff?' He said, 'I'm just trying to help you out.' And I said, 'Well, I realize that, but I've never flipped, I've never lost a passenger, and I've never broken an oar. Why don't you talk to the guys who really need help?' And he looked at me and he said, 'You know, you're right.' And furthermore, he shut up. It was amazing, he actually shut up."

Even though Liz could stand up for herself, she, like many beginning boatwomen, sometimes went to bed with tears of hurt and frustration. I asked her why she thought it was sometimes difficult for women to be accepted; after all, Georgie had been guiding for years. Liz replied, "Georgie was a wild card. There's always room for a wild card as long as it's not the whole deck. One guy told me that when people came down the Canyon, they expected the adventure of a lifetime. And if a girl can do it, how big a deal can it be?"

So what made it worth the frustration in the beginning, and what keeps her down there? "I like to see people expanding their limits and recharging their batteries. Plus, I'm a scenery addict. So here I am in one of the seven wonders of the world, and it's my job to have a good time down here. It's really pretty hard to beat. The only thing I've found that beats it is running around taking pictures of more of the same."

Liz is also pursuing other careers with her characteristic determination. After trying in vain to explain her Canyon trips to friends up top, she bought a camera. "It was a communication tool. Then one day somebody called up and needed a picture of a rapid for their adventure travel magazine. They put it on the cover and sent me a check for $500. I thought, well, great. I could do some more of this."

Her father, a photographer, suggested that Liz take up wedding photography, but Liz follows her own route. "I hate weddings with a passion, and you won't catch me in the darkroom." Currently, Liz's photos have appeared in several adventure magazines and books. Her unique panoramic photographs—pictures you can almost walk into—have graced two billboards. Liz is also exploring other business ideas. "I want a house and I want some other stuff. That costs money, so I'll get some."

Although Liz takes obvious pride in being in control, she said, "I'm increasingly enjoying letting go of the control issue. It's an illusion anyway." When we talked about Granite Rapid, I began to suspect that something in addition to the surrounding beauty and passengers kept Liz coming back into the Canyon year after year.

Granite Rapid is a long line of unpredictable waves freight-training along a dark cliff in the Inner Gorge. No matter how well a guide plans it, no matter how nicely a boat enters Granite, the boat gets hammered as it is carried over and through this series of huge waves that break every which way. The river guide, just like the passengers, is basically along for the ride. I asked Liz if she liked Granite.

"I love Granite."

"Do you ever feel in control in Granite?"

"Never!" Liz declared gaily. And those hazel eyes of hers sparkled.

CHAPTER 5

Louise Teal

John Running

Scrawny and unathletic, I was a pretty unlikely candidate to break into Grand Canyon river guiding, the last bastion of the male river god. It wasn't that I was uncoordinated, but in the early 1960s, my high school essentially had no athletic programs for girls. My experience in the outdoors was next to nil, except for playing in the vacant lot across the street from our house in the San Francisco Bay area or gaping out the car window while my dad drove through various national parks. I flunked canoeing at Camp Augusta because I refused to memorize all the various parts of the boat. My goal in high school, outside of leaving home, was to become a fashion designer; but Dad talked me out of art school because he was afraid I would turn into a communist. "Try UCLA first," he said. So I did, joined a sorority, got married, and moved to Seattle.

But before all that, back in high school, my dad and I went on a commercial river trip through Glen Canyon. I cannot begin to describe the beauty of that place—there was no other canyon like it. It is under water now, thanks to Glen Canyon Dam. Lake Powell is not one-tenth as beautiful as what lies buried underneath. But in 1963, Glen Canyon was still there, and we paddled a canoe down that easy stretch of the Colorado River miles above Lee's Ferry. It is a good thing it was easy because, early each morning, our canoe shoved off before the river guides who were motoring the main group. We were terrified of coming up to a place called Hell's Crossing until we realized we were reading the map wrong—it was Hall's Crossing.

I remember sitting alone one evening on a smooth sandstone boulder by a side creek, with a T-bone steak dripping in my hands. As I watched the swallows work the creek and the sun set salmon colors on the cliffs, I thought, this is the way to live. I want to keep doing this.

Too soon, the trip was over, and I was back to my real life—puberty, high-school trauma, and college plans. But I guess your soul has a way of remembering what you wish for, and things have a way of working out.

Years later—when I was living in Seattle, working as a secretary, married to a stockbroker, and sick to death of gray skies—I saw a National Geographic article about river trips through the Grand Canyon. Yes! I signed us up for $350 each. When the time came for the trip, my husband, Roger, couldn't leave because the 1970 stock market was so bad.

I went anyway, a passenger on a thirty-three-foot motor rig. It did not matter how big those boats were; the rapids looked huge and scared me to death. Even so, I loved being down there. The Canyon was beautiful and intense, a completely fulfilling place to be. I wanted to stay. But it did not sound like women worked down there except as assistants to their boyfriends or husbands. No matter: I was still operating from that old frame of mind that you married what you wanted to do. I would just convince my husband to become a boatman.

That was the easy part; he was ready to leave, so we headed south back to the sunshine. Roger wrote various outfitters for work, but none were interested in hiring a stockbroker to run boats. Then Robert Elliott of ARTA wrote back saying that he was running ARTA's first whitewater school and to "Come along!" (for a price, of course). The next year, 1972, Roger was running motor rigs down the Grand Canyon, and I was working as his assistant, a soul in bliss.

Our marriage was not to last much longer, but I had found my true love—the river and the Canyon. I had not yet found my boat, though. I never really warmed up to those motors. The next summer, I learned to use oars on the Stanislaus River in California. Roger and I purchased a raft and helped three other boatmen run free river trips for kids. A few wide-eyed juvenile delinquents paid their debt to society as my boat careened down that rocky river. At the end of that summer, Roger went fishing in Alaska for the winter, and I managed to get on another Grand Canyon trip, a snout-boat trip.

A tousled boatman let me row his boat some, and kind of like Tom Sawyer let Huck Finn paint the fence, he allowed me to catch the eddy below Blacktail Canyon. Eddies are necessary to catch in order to stop on shore. Some of the eddies in the Canyon are huge. In fact, some sections of the Colorado River have more water swirling upstream than current flowing downstream. A few infamous eddies even have names: King Edward, Ever-Eddy, Helicopter Eddy. Rowing into or out of an eddy through the "eddy fence" (a line of small whirlpools where the current is going every which way) can be tricky business if the current is particularly intense. And rowing across a wide eddy fence could be an ordeal in those old heavy snout boats.

Anyhow, the boatman grinned at me while I learned what "busting a gut" meant as I spent at least five minutes rowing through the eddy fence at Blacktail. While my spindly arms pulled on the thirteen-foot oars, he said to me, "If you can make this eddy, you could row the Canyon."

I made the eddy.

But it was more than just the willpower to catch that eddy that started me rowing down there. It was Robert and Jessie, the progressive owners of AZRA. And it was all the boatmen, especially my ex-husband—they were totally supportive. After talking with some other boatwomen, I realize now how lucky I was. Some did not have such an easy time of it, and they always felt under pressure to prove themselves, to always have excellent runs through rapids. But that really wasn't the program back then. As one old boatman put it: "I was really into trying to do good runs, you know, be a hot boatman. But the more trips I did, I realized that no one cared about how hot I was. In fact," he grinned, "the heroes were the guys with the wild-ass runs and the great stories."

Those boatmen were almost heroes to me in that they were some of the most clever, capable, giving, and funny people I had ever met. Now I will not say these guys never gave me a hard time. "Well," one boatman said, "we used to give you shit about Lava Falls just to get your goat, but I don't think it was because you were a woman. We razzed everyone about something, and yours happened to be Lava Falls, because you'd twitch when you got there."

As you might expect, there had to be a nightmare among all the dream-filled Canyon days. And for me it involved my old "twitching spot," Lava Falls.

I am still not sure what woke me up. Perhaps it was the odd movement of the snout boat I was sleeping on. What I saw when I peeked out from underneath my tarp made me nauseous. Even in my drowsiness, I realized I had just awakened to a river guide's nightmare—something we had always joked about as a possibility, but that had never happened. That is, not until that moment: the boats had somehow broken loose from shore, and I was floating downriver at night toward Lava Falls.

Lava Falls, that infamous rapid at Mile 179. After miles of quiet, flat water, it sounds like a 747 jet taking off. Lava pounds, heaves, and froths. Its thirty-seven-foot drop is full of small waterfalls, huge waves, holes, ledges, a folding V-shaped wave, and black lava rocks. Any number of these are capable of flipping twenty-two-foot boats. A windsurfer friend who regularly rides over waves clinging to a flying piece of fiberglass told me that riding through Lava Falls as a passenger was the ride of his life.

If we had been more careful how we tied up the boats that night, I would not have a story to tell. But we had been rowing against the wind for eight hours straight and had to stop, exhausted, a couple of miles above Lava. It was all we could do to cook dinner for twenty people, let alone remember details such as tying our boats to tamarisk trees large enough to hold in any change of water or wind conditions. But luckily, we only tied two of the boats to each other, instead of all three.

After the dishes were done, the wind continued to blow, and dark clouds gathered up the Canyon. I headed for the security of the boats to set up a rain shelter. After battling the wind for control of my plastic tarp, I dove under just in time to miss the first raindrops. Soon, I was listening to a full-blown Southwestern storm while being rocked to sleep by the river.

While I slumbered, the water rose (it fluctuates daily due to releases from upstream Glen Canyon Dam). Increasingly stronger current and wind moved the boats back and forth, slowly uprooting the pathetic little bushes holding the boats.

Finally, the roots gave way, and the rafts surged out into the current.

That's when I woke up, peered out from beneath my tarp, and realized I was in the middle of the Colorado River heading toward Lava Falls. I did what any girl who can't whistle would do—I screamed. Was anyone awake at camp to hear me?

I wasn't just careening downstream on one boat, but two twenty-two-foot snouts tied together. I quickly squirmed out of my sleeping bag and grabbed my life jacket first, then my channel locks and knife. My rain tarp was tied to my oars and raft frame. I needed to dismantle my temporary shelter enough to get oars in the water and a seat to row on. I cut the bowlines, because they were still attached to uprooted tamarisk trees that were now functioning as sea anchors. I didn't want anything keeping me in the current. I wanted to get to shore.

It was wild. Thunder, rain, lightning, and me, naked except for my life jacket, heading toward Lava. Whenever the lightning flashed, I could see enough of the canyon walls to know how close I was getting to Lava. I had flipped boats there in the daylight; I didn't figure my chances were good of getting through with two boats in the dark.

However, I did spend one moment imagining eternal glory in the river-guides' annals if I made a midnight run through Lava. Lightning flashed, and that vision was replaced with a more realistic picture of the boats hitting the first wave and sandwiching me between two snout rigs. Getting this floating disaster to shore seemed like a better idea.

The two boats, tied together at the bows, were being held side-by-side by the current, making it impossible to use both oars. I turned the boats several times with my one oar, but the current kept pushing the boats back together. I was cruising downstream fast: I needed both oars, and I needed an eddy.

Soaking wet, in the thunder and lightning with Lava Falls downstream, it was easy to think of God. Grateful that I was past my college atheist period, I asked for help.

The boats swung apart. In the next lightning flash, I could see a large eddy sparkling downstream. I dug in with both oars and headed for it. I broke through into the eddy, but that wasn't the end of it. The second boat was still in the downstream current and pulled my boat back out again. Downriver the boats went, while I tried to row both back into the eddy. It became a crazy dance in the water. One boat would get into the eddy, and the other would pull it out into the main current. The boats and I spun around. Depending on which boat was nearest the eddy, I pulled or pushed on the oars toward shore.

Finally, both boats were in the eddy. I rowed close to shore and grabbed at small willows to help me stop. When I could see a rock to tie to, I jumped off and wound a line around it. Not taking any chances, I tied the boats up to at least three rocks and two bushes. I was high on adrenaline and howled into the wind like a coyote. The storm was starting to move out. Of course, I forgot about thanking God and just felt great about getting the boats to shore all by myself.

My shivering reminded me that I was freezing, so I looked around for some clothes. I thought I would hike upriver and yell across to our camp, but as the adrenaline wore off and I looked at the rough terrain—prickly cactus and sharp travertine rocks—I thought better of that idea. Scrounging around for some calories to warm me up, I discovered our trip's supply of candy. "This is an emergency," I rationalized and ate as many M & M's as I could. After I rechecked my numerous lines tied to shore, I settled down in the boat to sleep.

As it turned out, someone did hear me scream when I made my unplanned departure from camp. A passenger had been up late gazing into the campfire. She was a bit puzzled by the boatmen's reactions when she woke them up: they spent the next five minutes rolling around in their sleeping bags, laughing hysterically. They gleefully pictured me sound asleep under my orange tarp floating toward the brink of Lava Falls.

I probably would have reacted the same. Finally, my ex-husband hiked downstream to look for the boats.

Again, I woke up. This time to someone shouting across the river and shining a flashlight my way.

"Is that you, Louise?" Roger shouted from the opposite bank.

"Yeah," I shouted back.

"How many boats do you have?"

"Two," I shot back. "How many do you have?"

"One," he replied.

I laughed across the river. "Well, I've got more than you!"

Eventually, I got tired of pushing those old snouts around and went somewhere I could row more responsive boats—working as a Grand Canyon National Park Service river ranger. It was a stellar crew that 1979 season, but even so, I am afraid I was too much of an anarchist at heart to work for the government. Plus, I really missed my old crew and the commercial passengers. By the end of the summer, I was back with AZRA. Fortunately, by then Jessie had convinced Robert that it was financially viable to row smaller boats—eighteen-foot rafts with ten-foot oars, rafts that could actually pivot.

No matter how river equipment, the river-tour industry, or

the Canyon changes, that ancient pile of rock never stops its song. And as one retired boatman said, "When you stick your oars in the water, you're feeling the whole story. There's no words, but it's the full language of the formation of the earth."

My life, too, is full of changes, but one thing that remains constant is coming back to the Canyon every summer, even if only for a partial season. It is an addiction that some people—employment counselors, my relatives, and a few mates—might say has been a curse. But to me, it has been my greatest blessing.

CHAPTER 6

David Edwards.

Susan Billingsley

"Susan was the best river-running partner I will ever know," said her husband, George. Susan Billingsley ran motor rigs with George for Ron Smith's Grand Canyon Expeditions from 1973 to 1976. When I talked with her in Flagstaff, Arizona, she looked like a classic cowgirl—western shirt and jeans, brown hair cropped short, and a deep, even voice sprinkled with humor.

Turned out she does spend a bit of time on horses—chasing coyotes. "It's a sport," she said, "like fox hunting, but we don't kill the coyote."

Susan grew up far from the Grand Canyon, in the Black Hills of South Dakota, running around with her older twin brothers. "They let me do everything with them: football, camping, hiking. It was a wonderful place to grow up. I just ran when I was a kid—I spent a lot of time out in the woods alone.

"I've been so comfortable working around men. I could always do what the men could do. I mean, sometimes there are physical challenges. On the river, when I picked up an engine, I had to have it up against me to be able to carry it."

With her background, it was no surprise that Susan wanted to work outdoors, or that she wasn't bothered when somebody told her she couldn't do something—like when she heard that the dean of forestry at Northern Arizona University (NAU) had said, "As long as I'm dean, no woman is going to graduate in forestry." As time went by, he changed his mind.

Susan said, "A lot of the guys in forestry didn't want me there. It just didn't fit their image of who they were. But I didn't feel like everybody should want me. I could understand why they felt that way, but that wasn't going to stop me from going through the program. I don't know why women would expect men to accept them unless they proved they can do the job. I mean, why should any guy accept with open arms a woman into a profession that he's worked hard to be in if he really believes she can't do the job?"

During college, Susan met her future husband. I asked her if it was ever a strain working on the river with him. "I was lucky in that my husband would rather run with me than anyone else. There were some other boatmen who didn't particularly want to run with their wives. No, it wasn't a strain, and you have to know my husband, he knows everything," she said, laughing. "But he isn't the least bit macho, he's just very competent in what he knows. He'll let you do anything you want, but if he feels it's better another way, he'll do it, and you can do it your way. That won't bother him at all. But," Susan added, chuckling, "his way was usually best. I kept thinking, well, I can do it *this* way, but pretty soon I'd realize that it was better his way. I don't know, maybe I'm just a born follower. I'm not pushy at all.

"But there's no way you can learn until you're on a boat by yourself. Because, when I was swamping in 1973, George would say, 'Okay, I'm not going to say anything, I'll be up in front of the boat.' But I could see him tense up at just the moment I was supposed to make a move with the boat. He wouldn't ever say anything, but I could just watch him and know exactly what to do.

"And I have to tell you this: my whole life, whenever I started thinking I was pretty good, something horrible has happened and just knocked the pins out of me. It's kept me from being a swellhead ever. On my first boat in 1974, I was going to run empty down to Lava. We got to the first rapid, Badger, and I just absolutely read the water wrong. I got stuck on that big rock right at the top. So there I sat as the water dropped. There was another Grand Canyon trip there, but even with ropes, there was no way they could get me off. So I spent the night right there on that rock, really embarrassed. All these other boat companies were coming by, and I sat there. It was just about the worst thing I could have done.

"A friend of ours had hiked into the Badger overlook, saw what happened, and went back and called Ron [the owner]. Ron's brother, Mark Smith, came down in a little sport yak. When he jumped on my boat, the sport yak got sucked underneath. That gave mine the buoyancy it needed and we were off in five minutes.

"On my second trip, there I was heading down to Badger again . . . Since I'd already had that fiasco there, I was really ready. I started into it, lifted up the motor for the first rock, then put it back in the water and started to drive—but my motor handle had broken off. My engine was going, but I didn't have a handle! I couldn't believe it! I got through all right and then changed it."

But more than running the river, Susan loved hiking and exploring the dry plateaus and many side canyons that make up the Grand Canyon. Floating through the Canyon, one's imagination can travel up to the plateaus, along the distant cliff walls, and out to remote pinnacles and monuments, but the actual immensity of the place cannot be truly appreciated until the distances and heights are measured on foot. Susan was vice president of NAU's hiking club, and one of their "unofficial" outings created a bit of a stir.

"We were going to hike down Mohawk Canyon, and nobody knew if you could do it. Dr. Butchart, a math professor who hiked and researched old trails, thought the Indians used to go down Mohawk Canyon and then cross the river to Stairway Canyon [Mile 171]. Butchart had heard that there was a way up and out Stairway, but he didn't know—nobody had done it. So two friends and I thought, ah, we will do it. We will do a three-day hike, take air mattresses, float across the river, and hike up and meet George and another friend on the north rim. George was going to be up there working on his geology master's thesis, mapping Tuckup Canyon.

"It was a total disaster; everything went wrong. It was one of those trips where, even though we made elaborate plans, nothing worked. Our truck got stuck up on the rim, and we had to walk in an extra twelve miles to the head of Mohawk Canyon. Then, we hiked eighteen miles down Mohawk Canyon in gravel. We ended up hiking thirty miles that day—leaving at midnight, hiking until four in the morning, sleeping for two hours, and hiking until five the next afternoon. Then, the next morning, during a climb down a ledge, a rock came loose and I fell fifteen feet and landed on my head. The rock came down on my shoulder. My friend, John, kept me from falling another twenty feet. I didn't break anything, but boy, did I have a headache. I'd gotten inflamed joints in my ankles from hiking in that gravel, so I couldn't bend them. They were just going 'grate, grate.' I was hobbling. There was no way I was hiking all the way back out Mohawk.

It was shorter to go across the river so we went on. We built rock cairns at the river (part of our elaborate plans), crossed the river, and hiked up Stairway. We had these firecrackers that we were going to signal George with.[1] They were going to wait for us until we got out of Tuckup Canyon [on] Monday night, if they heard the firecrackers. We made it up on top of the Redwall limestones, about a two-thousand-foot climb to the top, and lit a firecracker. We heard firecrackers, so we thought, all right, they heard us! So we lit another one off, and they lit another one off. Well . . . we knew then for sure that they knew we were there. There was no question in our minds.

"We hiked the next day, hiked and hiked. It was hot. We ate cactus apples because we were low on water. That made us sick. We got over to Tuckup Canyon where there was a spring. It was about another maybe 1,200 feet up to the rim and it was 9:00 P.M., Monday night. We were dying of thirst, so we drank that water, but it was full of gypsum alkali. I got even sicker. We made it out by 10:00 P.M., but nobody was there.

"Turned out, they had just happened to set their firecrackers off at the same time—they hadn't heard ours. And somehow, we'd miscommunicated about the time. Plus, they never really thought we could make it in the first place.

"We were stuck up there in the piñon-juniper forest for a whole week with nothing to eat but half a cup of rice and a spoonful of brownie crumbs, once per day for each of us.

"George had gone back to Flagstaff because he thought we'd never made it and were probably stuck out there on the south

1. The Park doesn't issue permits to swim across the river, nor does it approve of firecrackers.

rim. They drove all the way back through Flag and out to Mohawk Canyon and found our truck stuck in the mud. Then they hiked thirty miles down to the river to find out what happened to us. From our rock cairns at the river, they could see that we made it down and crossed the river, so they had to hike all the way back out.

"Well, classes at NAU had started by then, so they thought, we know exactly where they are, and we've missed two days of classes already; so we might as well stop and go to one class, then drive back to Tuckup Canyon to pick them up. But while they were in class, they happened to mention that we were 'missing,' and the geology professor said, 'Do you mean to tell me there's three people lost, and you haven't told the authorities?' And they said, 'We know where they are, we're just going to go pick them up.' But the professor insisted on calling in the authorities.

"It took two days for the sheriff to get up there to pick us up. By the time they had sent an air search out and got all the search and rescue people together, we had hiked out of Tuckup and headed north to Kanab.

"We had sat there for two days and decided we better get out of there; we were hungry. So we started hiking out, but we didn't have maps of the country north of the rim and weren't sure exactly which way would get us out the quickest. We could see planes all that week going up and down the Canyon. It turns out they thought we had drowned. Nobody ever came over to where we were supposed to be, and we were lighting these huge fires. For some reason, they wouldn't let George and his friend out of their sight to come pick us up.

"But when we were hiking, this plane finally saw us, and bingo, you know, they circled two or three times, and then along came seven search-and-rescue vehicles at ninety miles per hour. They almost ran us over. We had to jump off the road so we wouldn't get hit."

After Susan ran her own boat for three seasons, she and George decided it was time to raise a family, although both admit that he was more ready to quit the river than she was. For boatwomen, the choice to have children has also meant choosing to leave the river. Today, George works for the U. S. Geological Survey and Susan manages a river-supply store in Flagstaff. Unfortunately, she has had to stop backpacking because she has had some disk problems and cannot carry a pack now. According to her husband, "lifting those Mercury 20s [engines] on the river may have taken a toll on her back." Susan added, "A lot of the male boatmen have terrible backs too; it's not just women. Nobody in their early twenties would even begin to be careful about something like that. You can't foresee that you're going to have problems. You don't even know what back trouble is."

Susan, who never was much for regulations or crowds, thinks things have changed too much for her to ever want to work commercial trips again. "I suppose for the boatmen now, it's special too. A lot of it hasn't changed, but enough has for me. And looking back, hiking in the Canyon was more important to me than being on the river. The river is, after all, such a tiny piece of the Grand Canyon. And most of the river-trip side hikes are walking up streams, and that's not what the Grand Canyon is either. Our hiking explorations were really special, because even if I wanted to hike again now, I could never get that back. For one thing, it's more crowded. We probably couldn't get the backcountry permit dates, the Park Service wouldn't let us go in, we would get caught now.

I remember the last couple of years that we hiked, we'd see tour planes and helicopters. When we used to hike off the main trails, we never saw anybody, but toward the last we would run onto somebody or see footprints, and it would ruin it."

But still, Susan's eyes lit up whenever she talked about the Colorado, so I had to ask her, "Do you miss the river?"

"If I got close to the river and smelled it . . . if I was there, I would love it, I know. But I don't get down there."

CHAPTER 7

High Water of 1983

The high water of 1983 was a historic time—an intense experience common to most boatwomen in this book. This unusually high water is the backdrop of many stories in the next chapters, which will profile women who began running boats throughout the later 1970s.

Any feelings that early guides might have had about missing the 'good old days' when the Canyon seemed wilder were erased when we felt the river begin to rise. Certainly any remaining doubts about women handling boats, especially rowing boats, in powerful water should have been put to rest, as women worked and led trips during the high water.

Prior to the dam's construction, there had been even bigger runoffs, but there were fewer trips on the water. During the unplanned runoff after the dam was built and in the following high-water years, full-season guides consistently, trip after trip, faced the challenge of a high, fast Colorado. Yet it was a time when, as one boatwoman said, "our spirits were high," because none of the post-dam river guides had ever seen the river they loved run much over 50,000 cfs. (The flow usually fluctuated between 2,000 and 29,000 cfs.)

Before 1983, it seemed as if each river company was a separate tribe floating downriver—each with its own stories, traditions, and nicknames for places. And each group had its prejudices about which was the better way to see the Canyon, by motorboat or oar boat. But the high water of 1983 changed all that. No matter what type of boat they were running, all the guides felt pretty small next to the force of the Colorado. We needed each other's support. More than that, we all shared the thrill of watching the river show its true power.

The fellows at Glen Canyon Dam had miscalculated a little, or rather, nature did its usual trick of not always behaving like people think it will. The winter of 1982–83 was comparatively dry in the central Rockies, but there were unanticipated heavy snows in May, followed by unexpected warm weather that quickly melted the snowpack. This huge runoff headed down from the Rockies and was joined by the runoffs from the Wind River Range in Wyoming, the Uinta Mountains in eastern Utah, plus a few tributaries out of northern New Mexico. The runoff continued to build volume and energy, culminating in a total of approximately 100,000 cubic feet per second heading for Lake Powell and the cement plug keeping it all in, Glen Canyon Dam, fifteen miles above Lee's Ferry.

The dam is set up to release about 33,000 cfs through the turbines while it makes electricity. In addition to the 33,000 cfs through the turbines, about 20,000 cfs can flow through bypass tubes near the base of the dam. But this still wouldn't be enough to handle the flows the Colorado is capable of: 120,000 to 200,000 cfs during spring runoff. That's where the spillways are supposed to help—two forty-one-foot, S-shaped tunnels dug into the soft Navajo sandstone on either side of the dam. If there's more water than the turbines and bypass tunnels can handle, the lake will start spilling over and out the spillways, just like water going out a bathtub's overflow drain.

Only it didn't work that way when the runoff came down

in the spring of 1983. It wasn't just clear lake water flowing out of the spillways. Chunks of red sandstone, pebbles and boulders, piled up below the spillways. Something was terribly wrong. It looked like the spillways were breaking apart inside. As one boatman who went to see the dam described it, "Everything around there seemed to be vibrating, the whole ground shook."

Rumors were flying. How high would the water go? Would the dam break?

Below the dam, in the Canyon, the river kept rising—60,000 cfs, 70,000 cfs, and finally, on June 29, it peaked at 92,600 cfs. We were beside ourselves. We loved this river, and none of us had ever seen it approach its true glory. As one boatwoman said, "This was the most exciting time of our lives."

Actually, Georgie and a few others had seen such high water; they had run the river before the dam was built. One morning, as the river continued to rise, an official Park Service vehicle, with lights and sirens going, screamed down to the Ferry, and a ranger jumped out. He said that he needed to have a meeting with the boatmen—the Colorado River was closed. An older outfitter who was about to push off was a bit upset. Hell, he'd rafted the Colorado's flooding waters before most rangers at Lee's Ferry had even heard of river trips.

Still, everyone was concerned about the water rising. Outfitters held meetings, the Park held meetings, guides held meetings. Park helicopters dropped notes down to groups on the water, warning notes wrapped in little plastic bags weighted with gravel or rice. Boatmen read announcements such as, "63,000 released this morning—camp high—be careful." There were official assurances that everything was under control, that the water would not get any higher. More notes such as this were dropped: "70,000 released this morning—four motor boats and numerous oar boats flipped in Crystal—ninety people in the water—one fatality, fifteen injuries—passengers must walk Crystal—check in at Phantom [Mile 88, where there's a ranger station]."

The water kept coming up. Boats continued to flip. During the rise, somewhere around 60,000 cfs, AZRA decided to do an "exploratory," a trip with only boatmen to decide if we wanted to take passengers on the high water. I was on the lower half of the trip. The crew on my prior scheduled trip had been rearranged and I had been canceled, so I didn't answer my phone for a week for fear they would cancel me again. I figured if I showed up at the warehouse, I would get on that high water no matter what. After our exploratory, we decided we could run a commercial trip at 60,000 cfs, so we put on the water. On that trip, the river kept rising and finally peaked at 92,600!

During the high-runoff trips we rode on water like we had never seen before. We were on the edge of control. It wasn't like we were rowing our boats down the river; it was more like getting on a wild horse and hanging on. Whirlpools and eddy fences sucked our tubes down. Eddy fences along the sides of rapids were violent enough to flip boats, eliminating the option of avoiding the high, breaking corkscrew waves in the center.

There was no calm flat water. All the current was alive—swirling, folding, sucking, and moving incredibly fast, almost fifteen miles per hour. Huge unpredictable boils and whirlpools appeared and disappeared. The river was at least twenty feet higher than we had ever seen. Floating debris, old driftwood stuck on shore since the gates of the dam had closed twenty years before, sped downstream.

We floated past new pour-overs in places where we remembered only giant midstream boulders. We rode over riffles where we remembered major rapids, rapids now buried by the high water. We sped through Granite Narrows straining on our oars against the sideways currents that slammed from wall to wall. We floated by upside-down motor rigs tied to shore, their passengers long since evacuated. We floated into rapids on smooth tongues that swelled like the ocean. We learned to scout rapids a half mile upstream. That way, if the best place to enter the rapid was on the opposite side of the river, we would have time to row across the swift current. We couldn't keep our boats too close together or they'd ride up dangerously on each other. We couldn't stay too far apart, or before we knew it, we would be miles apart, unable to help each other. We portaged and lined rapids—something we had only read about Powell and other old-timers doing. Most of our camps and usual stopping spots were now under water. Boatmen were missing pull-ins, getting surged back out into the current on giant eddy-fence boils. A few boats even missed the take-out at Diamond Creek and had to float for two more days to the next take-out on Lake Mead.

But the climax to the high water and the location of many river stories was at Crystal Rapid, Mile 98, where big thirty-seven-foot motor rigs flipped end-over-end in the colossal breaking wave, or hole, that stretched across two-thirds of the river. Some people swam for miles before they could get to shore. Georgie's giant G-rig started making sense again, but even it almost went over in Crystal.

Since a flash flood of 1966 had created this rapid, we were hoping that the high water would clear a few boulders out. But to everyone's horror, Crystal became worse. The long smooth tongue that seemed to move at sixty miles an hour led to nowhere you wanted to go—except maybe in your dreams—the ones where you can fly like a duck and take a last-minute exit before you hit the Hole or any of its neighbors. All of them were eddies in some other terrible dimension, piles of water that mushroomed and surged, folded over and hammered down at eighty tons per second. The biggest, the Hole, was forty feet wide and thirty feet high. As one boatman put it, following the tongue down into Crystal's Hole would be like choosing to walk into a helicopter rotor. And waiting for you below churned a pinball swim through that spread of pour-overs and boulders called the Rock Island.

Terry Brian, a muscular, bearded OARS boatman and Park Service ranger at the time, was scouting the rapid when he saw the "old woman of the river, Georgie" and the new Crystal meet each other for the first time. Terry said, "It was the first time this hydraulic jump [the Hole] existed, period. It was steep, brand new, and just forming as we watched. That's when we saw Georgie coming down; her other boats weren't around. She saw what was happening downstream, reached down, and turned off her motor; then she got her hands into those wrist loops she had to hold on . . . and her rig went right into the wave. That wave broke over top of her thirty-seven-foot rig and just shoved her down. And the boat sat there. And it surfed."

His wife Nancy, a scientist who also rows, added, "It buckled and sprung back up, and when it did that, people and bags just flew. It did that three times, and the last time there wasn't anything but Georgie left on the boat."

Terry said, "We were watching thirty people going downstream."

Nancy added, "And we had to run it next."

Remembering the whole scene, they looked at each other and chimed, "Park Service to the rescue."

And rescue people they did—thankfully, all before the next rapid around the corner. And Georgie? When they talked to her later, she uttered her now-infamous line: "Well, I told them to hang on. They don't make passengers like they used to."

There would be other flips and other rescues before the water dropped. The eroding spillways were shut down before they destroyed the dam. Sheets of plywood were hastily erected to increase the dam's holding capacity and prevent water from pouring into the spillways again. Fingers were crossed, prayers were uttered, and there were many official sighs of relief when the runoff from the mountains finally subsided.

The water in the Canyon also subsided, but for the next few years, it was still high and wild, almost too wild at Crystal and Lava. "The terror years" was what one boatwoman called it. Another boatman, who has been avidly running rivers for twenty years, was overheard to say at Crystal, "I wish I'd never even heard of river running."

Boatwoman Suzanne Jordan recalls seeing a boatman from another trip flip in Crystal when she was scouting for her run: "He didn't do a traditional flip. When he hit the wave it broke, as erratically as it could have broken, like the worst break ever. He threw his body on the downstream tube [attempting to prevent a flip] and it threw him up in the air. He was overboard hanging onto the bowline. Then the wave pulsated again and threw him back in the boat. Then it pulsated again and threw him over the side. Then it threw him back in the boat. The boat went up in the air in a flip and threw him into the river, back in the hole, and then just threw the boat in on top of him. And we stood watching. Not only were we just getting sick, we were standing up on top of the high hill with all of our paddling passengers, who were just fixing to get in their boats and paddle through. After that, two out of the next five boats flipped. Martha [another river guide] turned to me—and there were tears in my eyes and there were tears in Martha's eyes—and she said, 'I think we'll line.' " The flipped boatman managed to crawl up on the bottom of his boat. He passed out, but his boat surged safely into an eddy below where another boat picked him up.

Most of the time, oar boats made it past those holes. If not, the flips were usually a bit less traumatic. But it was "iffy," you didn't always know. As another boatwoman named Fritz said, "We just went out there and took our beatings." Even so, many guides felt the nausea before Crystal was well worth having the high, fast water because that gave trips so much more time for hiking and exploring the Canyon. Still, everyone seemed pretty glad when, after a few years, the water dropped again. But most guides who rode on the highest water wouldn't have missed it for the world. Every boatman and boatwoman can tell you exactly where they were when the Colorado peaked in the spring of 1983.

One boatwoman said something that would have amused Georgie but shows how quickly the present becomes history. "The old timers used to be the ones who saw the low water in '77, and now the old timers are the ones who saw the high in '83." Suzanne Jordan, the next woman profiled, was one of those old timers.

CHAPTER 8

Suzanne Jordan

David Edwards. Color slide.

Suzanne Jordan is an extremely competent, solid lady with long thick hair the color of fire and a continually peeling, freckled nose. Her sweet southern voice could charm a rattlesnake back into its hole. Suzanne quickly became a trip leader or, as we used to call it at AZRA, head boatman. She has traveled the world, worked many exotic rivers, and one season, managed an Utah river company. While her southern charm can be handy in getting things done, it is her practical sense that earns her respect.

"Suzanne has down-to-earth intelligence—an ability to look right at the root of a problem and fix it," said a fellow Canyon guide. "I really saw that when we were putting together trips overseas in Africa.

"It's a commonsense thing. One time on the Colorado, a girl had twisted her ankle up Havasu Canyon, and we carried her back to the boats. Along the way, a branch jabbed into her ear and pulled back out again. It pulled some stuff out with it—a strand of thick red globulous stuff. We are thinking, well, her eardrum has been yanked out.

"We're trying to figure it out. I was all for—leave it alone, put a pad on it, and fly her out. Another guide said, 'Well, what if it's no big deal? What if her eardrum is okay. Let's look and see.' So we got a flashlight and were looking down into her ear to see if the strand was connected, when Suzanne walked up and asked what's going on.

"After listening to us, Suzanne put her finger in this girl's good ear, leaned towards the girl's injured ear, and said, "Can you hear me talking?"

Another boatwoman told me how impressed she was with Suzanne's sensitivity. "We got this guy way the hell up Elves Chasm; he was scared to death of heights, but none of us had picked up on it except Suzanne. She knew that he was terrified and wouldn't make it down. Suzanne went up and sort of enveloped him, which was very foreign to me. I'd never worked with anybody who was like her—that sort of mother figure, that leadership woman thing. It was incredible. In that southern, seductive way, she led him down out of there. I just watched, flabbergasted."

"You know," Suzanne said, "I used to go down the river, and I'd look around at my passengers and think, these people don't really know who I am. I should be somebody's mom in Alabama. I should be canning tomatoes and having people over to my house for Christmas dinner. But instead, I'm down here rowing this boat. I was so out of what I thought was my character that, even though I loved what I was doing, I thought that I must have failed somewhere in my life."

When she was twenty-one, in the spring of 1972, Suzanne came out west to visit her boatman brother who worked for ARTA. He managed to get her on a Museum of Northern Arizona river trip. Suzanne said, "I was like Alice in Wonderland, in awe of the whole thing. I asked every dumb question in the book. I mean, I thought the Grand Canyon was in a drought, and the river should have been up to the top.

"They'd say, 'We're going to hike over there and have lunch.'

It would be like 1,500 feet, and I'd go, 'Give me a break. I couldn't get there in two days.'

"But meeting those guys, the early ARTA boatmen and museum crew, was the best thing in the world. They just took this little sister's hand and said, 'Come on, we're going to take you with us, and you're going to go places.' And I did it because they had so much faith in me that I wasn't going to let them down."

The boatmen added the direction Suzanne felt was missing in her life. Her dad had died before she was born. Suzanne believes her drive and inner strength comes from her mom, who had to start her life all over again while raising two children. "My mom used to say you just have to take a deep breath and go on."

After assisting on quite a few Canyon trips, Suzanne asked Robert Elliott if she could work, but he told her to come back after she had more experience. (His wife and co-owner, Jessie, admits that they were still nervous back then about having too many women on the crew.) Later, in 1977, after working in California, Oregon, and Idaho, Suzanne walked back into Robert's office and declared, "Well, I'm back." She has worked in the Canyon ever since, about 120 trips now, half of them in paddle boats where the guide rudders from the back and directs six paddlers. The art of captaining a sometimes nervous crew through intense rapids or inspiring a tired crew during days of constant upstream winds has to be experienced to be truly appreciated.

Suzanne said, "I get a helluva lot from those people I take down. They love me without me even doing anything." She laughed. "I mean, give me a break; it's easy. I'm only doing what those first boatmen did for me."

It is arguable that people love her "without her doing anything." As trip leader, particularly, she is always concerned, always thinking. There is the schedule: Should we hike here? Will it flash flood? What are the other trips on the water doing? Will that camp be open? When is the high-water release from the dam coming? Will we have time to hike here and still make it down to camp before dark?

And there are the people from varying backgrounds. Suzanne watches each passenger. She knows they are ultimately responsible for making themselves happy, but she also knows she can enhance their happiness. She makes sure people are comfortable at their own individual levels. "Some people enjoy a challenge; some would freak out and will gain more just sitting under a tree or slowly strolling up a side canyon."

And she watches her crew. "The trip is only as good as the support of the crew. But we're not really in control of the trip, the Canyon is.

"It's the place," Suzanne said softly. "It just wraps its arms around you." She reminisced about what she loves about the Grand Canyon—the aromatic scent of sand verbena, the smell of rain coming in the distance, the smell of silt in the mudwater, the water ripples reflecting orange and purple at sunset, the moon casting a silhouette of the Canyon rim on the opposite side of the river.

"The Canyon is my sanity," she said. "It's a meditation that most people don't get in their lives. A Japanese man who spoke little English once told me, 'When I came on this trip I thought I was going to be really lonely. And you know, I *enjoy* being lonely, being alone sitting by the river just looking at the water. This is the Japanese way. For the first time in my life, I feel Japanese.' "

But a river trip is not always a tranquil meditative experience. For instance, take what happened to Suzanne at 24-1/2 Mile Rapid right after the 1983 peak. The river, flowing fast between the boulder-jumbled shores, takes a sharp turn to the left as it enters 24-1/2. The water was still high, about 60,000 cfs or so, when both she and Martha Clark, another boatwoman, flipped in 24-1/2.

David Edwards, a strong six-foot-plus boatman, described entering the rapid on that trip. "The waves were breaking every which way cattywampus. I hollered at my people to high-side [to throw their weight to the downstream tube in waves to prevent a flip]. I got knocked all over, but I made it through. I shouted to the passenger behind me to look back at the boats coming behind us. 'Suzanne's over!' he shouted. I told him to look for Martha's boat. 'She's over too!' he said."

When David saw Suzanne again, it was below the next rapid, 25 Mile. It looked like she had jumped on someone's upright boat, tied the two flipped rafts to it, and was rowing all three boats to shore. David said, "I had a hard time rowing one boat to shore at 62,000 [cfs], and here she was pulling two upside-down boats to shore."

Quite a bit had happened to Suzanne in that swirling, muddy water before David saw her rowing those boats.

Suzanne said, "I'd gone into this big breaking wave in 24-1/2, buried myself in it, and came out upside down. I thought I went into it straight. You know, like we always do." Suzanne laughed hard, throwing her head back and crinkling up her sunburned nose.

Then she was serious again, saying softly, "I came up under the boat, and I was really calm, even though I couldn't breathe. I just felt around with my hands over my head. Okay, I told myself, I'm going to start going out from under the boat now. But we went into another wave, and I was trapped. The boat was pinching me somehow, holding me under. We went into another wave, and I reached up again and swam, but I was still trapped somehow. You know how we used to hang our spare oars on loops? Well, I had swum out between the boat and the spare oar, so I couldn't get all the way out. But that was the first time I got air. Then, I had to go back underneath the boat again to get out." All this is happening as the boat is tossing and spinning through the roaring rapid. And the next rapid, 25 Mile, is coming up fast.

"Finally, I was pulling myself up onto the bottom of the slippery boat. I didn't even look around to see if anybody else was swimming because I was just trying to breathe, trying to save my own life. I'm halfway up on the boat when I heard this 'whimper, whimper.' I looked over my shoulder and there was Joyce, this plump schoolteacher, floating in the water.

"So I started easing myself back into the water and swam over to her. I remember her saying, 'Suzanne, I'm scared to death.' And here we were entering—I mean, we were in the tongue of 25 Mile Rapid—and I said, 'Joyce, there's nothing to be afraid about now.' Because there wasn't. We've always said that swimming rapids is only water." And Suzanne laughed her crazy laugh again.

She managed to haul herself and Joyce back onto the upside-down boat before the waves of 25 Mile. Then, they looked around and saw more swimmers nearby. Suzanne pulled more people up, and they all rode through the rapid clinging to the flip line, which runs along the bottom of the boat.

Eventually, all the boats and people were safely on shore. The boatmen saw to it that the passengers were warm, dry, and comfortable. Suzanne treated one woman for shock.

"We'd done everything, and I turned to David and Martha

and said, 'Let's go for a walk before we turn the boats back over.' We walked down the beach; David put his hand on my shoulder, and tears just burst out of my face. I told them that I'd almost died trapped under the boat. Then, I took a deep breath, and we went back and turned the boats right-side up.

"I'd lost all my bracelets during the swim, about six Hopi bracelets and one with this eagle on it. It symbolized, you know, the eagle and flight and freedom. It must have got caught in a strap or something because, when we flipped the boat right-side up, there, right in the middle of my rowing seat, free as anything, was that eagle bracelet.

"But," Suzanne said in a tone that makes you want to cuddle and obey her all at once, "you're not just going to tell about disasters, are you? It's such a small part of what's happening down there."

That is definitely true, but the occasional flips, the disasters and near disasters, are a big part of the stories that are passed around. And what happened on Suzanne's trip at Havasu, when her quick thinking saved a life, is one of those stories.

River trips usually stop at Havasu, mile 157, where Havasu Creek glows blue-green as it passes between the limestone narrows at the mouth of Havasu Canyon. One day in July 1984, two AZRA trips, about ten boats, were tied in the small alcove at the mouth. The day had started off typically sunny and gorgeous, so everyone headed up the creek for a day of fun. Walt Disney could not have designed a better playground, but it is not Disneyland. Things can happen. For one thing, it is a desert canyon, and like all desert canyons, it is subject to flash floods.

Later that day it started to rain. Soon the sky turned black, and it started to hail. When that outburst passed, it kept on raining. Many passengers and boatmen were on their way back down the creek from a day's hiking, but some, including Suzanne, were already back and sitting near the boats. Two boatwomen on the boats heard "an ever-so-slight change in the sound of Havasu Creek." They yelled, "Flash flood!" and before another guide had finished saying, "No, it's not," these boatwomen were running across the boats for shore. Within seconds, a flood was pushing a wave of clear water out the narrow gorge, followed by a three-foot wall of muddy water and debris.

The boatman whose boat was tied nearest Havasu's mouth stood on one tube of his boat trying to keep it from flipping in the flood. Bowlines, stressed taut as sling-shots, started to snap. Bam, bam, bam! They sounded like gunshots. The rock wedged in a slot holding the boats broke into pieces as the rope pulled out. Rocks flew through the air. It was like a war zone. As most of the boats started to surge out of the eddy and into the river, someone yelled, "There's a body going under the boats!"

When the body, a woman, resurfaced, boatman David Edwards jumped into the boiling river after her. David grabbed her, but he was being swept out into the high-water Colorado.

David said, "We were being washed along the wall. Another boatman was running real low to the ground, almost in a squat, trying to grab my hand. But I was being washed out into the middle of the rapid.

"All of a sudden I heard Suzanne yell, 'Daaivee, look this way!' She threw the throw-bag [rescue line] to me, right on top of me. Everybody says I jumped in and saved that woman, but it was Suzanne throwing that line. She's always spot-on and one of the bravest people I've ever worked with down there."

CHAPTER 9

Tim Lawton. Color slide.

Becca Lawton

"You know, I've done a lot, but there's been nothing like holding those oars in my hands and putting my boat exactly where I wanted it. Nothing. I love reading water. It's intellectually stimulating. People have no idea how much we row with our brains.

"I remember above some monster rapid a boatman was talking about praying to the river gods to let us through. And I said, 'No, it's nothing to do with the river gods, you just have to put your boat in the right place.' "

Becca could definitely row. She was "a superlative oarsman," said Jessie. "I've never seen Becca screw up or look rattled by a run, ever. And yet I know she's a very fragile, sensitive person. How she managed to look like she was always in control beats the heck out of me."

"My parents never gave me a sense that I was limited to anything," Becca said. "I overheard my dad once telling people that I always wanted to be as fast as the boys. That never occurred to me. I just always wanted to do the neat things they were doing. If they were going off in a boat to Rattlesnake Island to look for arrowheads, I was not going to stay back and play with dolls."

Even when Becca was keeping up with the guys or wearing one of her smashed and smudged billed caps, it was impossible for her not to look feminine with her lithe, slender figure and large liquid brown eyes. At first glance, Becca looks serious and intense, until something makes a big grin spread across her face. Often that something is her own fiery, quick humor.

Her river career probably started when her older river-guide brother took her on a Stanislaus River trip in 1972, back when she was sixteen. ("I liked the river immediately!") But her brother did not encourage her to become a guide, which she understood. "He had this thing he was doing, and who would want his little sister there? Plus, I wasn't really thinking, gosh, this is something I *must* do." That summer Becca worked as a soda jerk for Fred Harvey, a concessionaire on the rim of the Grand Canyon. The next year in college, a bird-watching boatman friend encouraged her to interview for a river-guide job on the Stanislaus. Hired on the spot by Ken Brunges, a California outfitter who believed in gender-balanced crews, Becca, at seventeen, began her career as a river guide. She transferred to working for ARTA halfway through the season. "I was really ambitious about getting on lots of rivers, and I knew ARTA would take me to other states."

In addition to working in California, where she rowed on the Stanislaus, American, and Tuolumne, Becca worked rivers in Utah and Idaho. "I thought I was pretty hot by the time I was finished with a year in California," she laughed. "I was sent up to Utah the next year because I was studying geology. They wanted somebody who was into rocks, and I was into rocks." She continued her education in the off-season, earning a bachelor's degree with honors in geology by publishing her research on ancient river deposits in Dinosaur National Monument. "That little paper on dinosaur bones in river sandstones is still sometimes used for field trips out there," she said, and grinned. "Being on the water all the time, we've got to know a little bit about how currents work."

Becca has a talent for writing, with words and with musical notes. She played the French horn in high school and studied jazz at the University of Utah. A soft feeling comes into her voice when she talks about her music. I remember listening to her sing and play her guitar under the stars in the Canyon. "A lot of the songs I've written have come right out of that place. Basically I picked up the guitar because that's what was happening on the river. I didn't want to sit inside playing the horn anymore."

When she sings, she has the voice of an angel. But that voice used to change pretty quickly if you made some snide remark about women. (She was not particularly fond of the term "hag.") There is an infamous Becca story that gets told at least once a year on the river.

Becca and I were sitting on the patio furniture outside her California apartment, and I reminded her of that story. "Yeah," she giggled. "Remember that article in that sports magazine? They had pictures of women guides smiling and looking noble, and what they wrote about me was what I said to this passenger. They softened it some, but it was the F-word.

"It was above House Rock Rapid. He was a little guy, and he'd been needling me all day. We were watching all the men ahead of us pull their snouts really hard to the right to miss the holes at the bottom. After he watched the boats, he looked at me, and he looked down at the rapid, and he said, 'God, honey, are you sure you can handle this?' So I told him what he could do with himself, and went through House Rock fine."

Becca said that she probably would have handled it differently now or at least been able to patch it up afterwards.

Even so, there were reasons for her to be sensitive to male harassment back then—she'd been through a lot as a pioneer commercial boatwoman on numerous rivers. In 1974 in southern Utah she was the only woman she knew to be rowing on any crew. "In Moab, Utah, I got my paranoia about being perfect, because if I ever screwed up it was the talk of Moab. Even if men had screwed up the same way, it would be in the bars, 'Well, that *girl* rowing for ARTA screwed up in Skull Rapid today.' So I got really defensive. I was young and not real capable of handling every kind of thing that came my way."

Becca enjoyed knowing that she was a pioneer, that she was proving that women were not too weak to row commercially. "They hired all these inexperienced men who were strong, but I could row circles around them, you know," she said, smiling brightly.

Eventually, Becca managed ARTA's northern Utah operation. In Idaho, she became the first licensed woman guide to row the highly technical Selway River. "When they told me I was going to the Selway, I remember thinking, well, yeah, it is my time to go. I hadn't thought, okay, I'm going to row the Selway, and you guys better let me go. I never said that. I just kept doing my job. With the previous Idaho manager, no women were going to get on the Selway, but when Guy Best started managing, it was, 'Okay, women are going!' And I was there, so I was the one. It was so neat because none of the other companies were even hiring women.

"I just wanted to be on the river all the time back then. I couldn't afford a raft, so I made a kayak just to go on rivers, and I'd kayak all winter until it was time to raft again.

"I heard about you [Louise] rowing the Canyon, and what did it, what made me go to the Canyon was that Randy [another boatman] said, 'They'll never let you row down there.' So I said, 'I'm going there, no matter what.' "

And she did. In 1976, when she was managing the Utah operation, Becca was invited to work an AZRA snout trip as an assistant. (That was how you became qualified back then, by rowing with a different guide every day for three trips.) Although many of the rivers where Becca had rowed were certainly more difficult, a long, hot Canyon snout-boat trip had its own demands. "I felt pretty determined to do something that hard physically day after day. You know the winds, those hot winds that dry your skin and make you feel old before your time. It's like a furnace down there. It was really a challenge. I went back to school and lifted weights all winter."

Becca rowed the Canyon for the next ten years. Although "being around those people felt more alive to me than I've felt anywhere," she still felt a little hassled by some of the guys—like when she was head boatman for the first time, and one crew member purposely rowed right on past the beach where Becca had stopped to set up lunch. Yet, looking back, she feels that "maybe a lot of it was just teasing and I took it as . . . I don't know. I had already gone through it big time in Utah; I didn't want to go through it again. I think I had as many problems from being young as being female.

"It was difficult sometimes. I remember this particular day in the Canyon when Upset Rapid was low and we were scouting it, trying to see about running right or running left. The guys were all over there discussing it, and here was my boyfriend (a Utah guide but a guest on that trip) standing with them. I felt just so . . . it was almost like there was a beacon coming down from the heavens that isolated me in this spot.

"I asked my boyfriend about it later, and he said, 'Well, we just think you're the sly old river fox, and you don't need our help.' I never thought I was on a different plane. I just thought I wasn't part of them. But I didn't want to be part of the boys, I wanted to be part of the crew. That was it."

"Could you have gone over and joined them?" I asked her.

"One would think so, but I don't know, I just didn't feel free. I'd been on crews where the boatmen would just turn their backs on you. Plus," she grinned, "there was nothing I wanted to ask them."

Maybe it wasn't only Randy's challenge that brought Becca to the Grand Canyon—part of her attraction for the area may have been in her genes. She felt a special closeness with her grandfather, who worked on geologic surveys of the Grand Canyon in the 1920s, especially around Tuckup Canyon (Mile 164). He also guided in the Adirondacks in upstate New York. "I feel like a lot of who I am came from him because he passed guiding down through my mother, who was an outdoor environmental teacher and the motor behind many of our family outings. When he died of cancer, I felt like his ghost was around me until a friend gave me some prayer feathers for my birthday. I took them up into Tuckup with some really nice passengers who helped me make the climb. I hung the feathers in a little alcove. After that, his ghost was gone, like his spirit finally said good-bye."

Another place that Becca (and others) feel is inhabited by spirits is the mouth of Nankoweap Canyon, which joins the Colorado right at Mile 52. Looking up Nankoweap Canyon, one can see a dark green line of pines on the distant rim. When the wind is just right, the scent of pine drifts down the canyon, following the same winding route that the "ancient ones" followed down to the Colorado River. The river sweeps around Nankoweap's large delta, which is dotted with Indian ruins. Relics and more ruins are tucked into high limestone caves above. Across the river, an almost vertical wall rises four thousand feet high, dramatically displaying each colored strata that the river has cut through.

"The changing light on the wall at Nankoweap is the prettiest sight I can remember," Becca said. "Even now when I need peace or inspiration, I travel in my mind to that wall. One time, on a trip I did in February, I saw a swan there. It was a tundra swan. Only a few come through in winter. I was walking away from the river when someone down the beach yelled my name. I turned to see this magnificent white bird passing by, all the whiter for flying by that red, red wall.

"Other bird things have happened to me at Nankoweap. A great horned owl visited me one night and perched on the log I was sleeping near (which I shouldn't have been because of scorpions). Because owls are sometimes interpreted as signs of death, it kind of gave me the creeps. But it was neat, too."

After the high water of 1983, Becca said good-bye to AZRA. "I felt like I was giving less and less to the passengers," she said. Like Marilyn, Becca disapproved of the party focus she felt some of the guides had then. But she loved rowing and was not ready to leave the Colorado.

"A career counselor gave me a test and advised, 'You should be doing the very thing you're doing, except with a group focused on education and research.'" Working as a Grand Canyon National Park Service river ranger seemed perfect because Becca loved to encourage people to protect our natural resources; plus, she could become involved in scientific research again. But she found that the Park "was having a trend toward law enforcement, and the resource was kind of getting a back seat." She also noticed that her rowing was "getting sloppy. I wasn't getting an adrenaline rush for anything. I knew it was time for me not to be there."

But before she left, she worked several National Park Service trips patrolling by kayak. "I think the most exciting thing I ever did was running Lava at 60,000 [cfs]. It was so smooth, it gets glassy at 60 [thousand]. I went over this wave, and it was like being in the ocean or something—coming down it was the most beautiful thing.

"I quit right after the high-water years, so that's what's still in my mind. Crystal at high water was just terrifying to me, and on another trip, having that guy drown there when we were on patrol didn't make me any more fond of the rapid. Actually, on my first year on the Stanislaus there were deaths, and I saw one. It was maybe my first month of working.

"But the thing at Crystal was so weird because I had met this guy right above the rapid. He was an older fellow on another trip, a private trip. We ran through first. I had just kayaked through at 50,000 cfs, one of the most thrilling runs of my life. I got knocked out into the middle and went through everything sideways and bracing. We were down below when we saw him floating by. He had his life jacket on but was floating low. I was the one who got to him first and pushed him to a raft to pull him out. For the next two hours we did CPR on him, but he was dead as a doorknob by the time we got to him. We didn't know for sure that he'd drowned in Crystal when we started thumping on his chest. That had me shook up for a little while." Becca had commented after the incident that it took a good bit of whiskey to wash the taste of death from your mouth.

Earlier on that same trip, miles above Crystal, "something shifted" in Becca's life. She paddled her kayak into an eddy on a routine Park checkout of a private trip and noticed a fellow in the shade just staring at her. She thought, "Why don't you take a picture. It'd last longer." But he was thinking, "Somebody important has just paddled into my life," which is pretty amazing considering Becca was almost completely covered up in the usual kayaking gear—baggy paddling jacket, helmet, and bulky life jacket.

She ended up talking with him for a couple of hours and found they had quite a bit in common. She was not quite ready for a life partner, but "I kind of set my sights. A couple of years later, I married him. I left the river the week before we got married, and I didn't go back."

Today, Becca writes for a living and is blessed with a daughter, a little curly-headed girl named Rose.

"Now, I'm on baby time. I'm on her schedule, like I was on the river's schedule, when days were measured by miles, and side canyons by hours, and things were slowed down to the very basics. I was living by the second hand after the river, but I've slowed down to watch and take care of her. It's an added blessing to having a child."

Of course, I had to ask her if she missed the river. "Every single day. Now that I've been off for five years and still can't forget it, I understand that I need to be on the water."

I looked out the window where Rose was playing in the yard. A brand new red canoe leaned up against the fence.

"I'm feeling like boating again, and that canoe is the way I'm going to do it. I feel like the rest will come from there, just like it came in 1973. I just followed what I wanted to do, rather than having a great plan, and it happened." She smiled and declared, "Maybe somebody will tell me again that I can't do something, and I'll do it."

I saw Rose grinning, a big smile like her mom's spreading across her face. She may not be able to talk yet, but she knew there was room for more than one in that red canoe.

CHAPTER 10

David Edwards. Color slide.

Connie Tibbetts

When Connie Tibbets isn't in the Canyon driving large motor rigs, she is either parachuting, flying her beloved 1947 Lascombe airplane, or operating commercial planes.

Quite a few years ago, between river trips, Connie and a few friends decided to drive to Yosemite and jump off El Capitan—just for fun. "Three steps and we were off," Connie said. "That's all there was room for.

"El Cap is like this: there's one rock, a slight overhang that kind of sticks out a little bit, and then it goes way down, I don't know, a thousand or maybe fifteen hundred feet. Then after that, there's talus. So when you jump off, you've got to get out a ways because otherwise you only have a thousand feet before impact. But if you get out past the talus, you can go all the way out, and then you have your full two thousand eight hundred feet.

"And you can't do it running. There's only a foot or so of room where you can jump, because there's a big rock behind you. And the slab you're on is sloping. I just remember standing there, my back against the wall, me and two other guys. Vern went first, I went second, and Al went last. You just take three steps and go for the biggest swan dive you can get.

"I watched Vern go and he somersaulted, but you don't

want to do that. You want to stay stable, and as soon as you feel the air, as soon as you've got enough air, you start bringing your hands back so you can get in a position to track away from the wall. You want to start moving out as quickly as possible. You have to track for ten seconds before you can pull. You're losing altitude, but you're also going out."

"You just tuck your arms to get away from the cliff. You take a position like this." And Connie demonstrated a taut, controlled forward slant, with her slim arms straight down by her side, and her hands cupped forward slightly.

"You can track out horizontal at sixty miles per hour away from that talus so that you can pull your parachute. Then if you have any problem, you can deal with it before you hit.

"The adrenaline is so good. It's kind of like running a rapid. You're thinking about what you're doing so you don't even know if you're scared or not.

"It took two and a half minutes maybe. The valley is so beautiful and so quiet, and your parachute opens and goes 'kraaack' and echoes through the whole valley. It's really cool.

"The sound woke up these climbers that were hanging off the face of the cliff in hammocks. They screamed at us as we went by, 'You guys are nuts!'

"It was one of those feelings where if you died right then, it'd be okay. You've lived long enough. You know what I mean?"

Connie's accent gives away her roots—upstate New York, where she spent a good deal of time out in the garage helping her dad fix up cars. In her home economics class, she added dead flies instead of chocolate chips to the cookie batter. She talked about her childhood as we walked along an abandoned dirt road behind her desert home near Lee's Ferry. She was dressed in baggy shorts and a loose summer top. Her blond hair was cropped straight across her shoulders, and her almond-shaped blue eyes twinkled under her bangs.

In an indirect way, skydiving was her mom's idea. Connie had liked the picture on NAU's college catalog. By fixing up and selling enough old cars, she earned the money to come out west to study industrial arts. Her mom suggested that Connie join lots of clubs at NAU in order to make new friends. Her mom probably never suspected where it would lead. "So I became a charter member of the Skydiving Club. It became a passion. I was learning more skydiving, so I blew off school. I'd go jump until I didn't have any money, and then come back to Flagstaff and work at the Monte Vista Hotel bar. They'd always put me on as a waitress, and in a couple of months, someone would quit and I'd bartend until I made a bunch of money and could go skydive again.

"This lady who owned the bar kind of took a personal interest in me; she took me aside and said, 'Hey, this life isn't good for you.' "

I asked Connie what the lady meant, the bar or the skydiving? She laughed. "The bar, of course. She encouraged me to meet her friends who owned this little trading post at Vermilion cliffs."

But Connie was happy with how things were. Besides, where was this Vermilion place anyway? As it happened, Connie soon received a phone call from a fellow named Myron who lived near the Vermilion Cliffs. He had heard that she was a skydiver. He was too, and he was hurt and needed a place to stay in Flagstaff before they would release him from the hospital. Could he stay at her place? While Myron recovered, he showed her pictures of the "baloney boats" (motor rigs) he ran down in the Grand Canyon. "I just wanted to throw up,"

Connie said. "I couldn't believe he thought it was neat to herd around tourists. I could never be close to that many people." When he left, he promised to show her around the Vermilion Cliffs area as a thank-you.

He came through on his promise, and one weekend ("I think it was in 1975") they four-wheeled around his home, which was not too far from Lee's Ferry, basically out in the middle of nowhere. ("I fell in love with the place.") They drove back into some wild, red slickrock country and eventually down to the Ferry to look at the Colorado.

When she was back working in Flagstaff, Fred and Carol Burke, owners of Arizona River Runners (ARR) and the small restaurant/motel/trading post at Vermilion Cliffs, walked into the Monte Vista bar. "They asked me if I wanted to come work for them up in Marble Canyon, and I said, 'Yeah!' I'd just been busting my butt getting a pilot's license and tending bar. I threw everything I owned in my car the next day and drove up to Marble Canyon to start my job. I cooked for the boatmen, and Fred gave me a couple of river trips as a swamper and . . . well, that was the end. History from there. I just wanted to come back and come back and come back, so I begged trips for jobs as a swamper.

"I worked really hard and tried to be a good employee for Fred, and I think that's why he let me be a swamper." Connie laughed as she remembered how it all happened. "At the end of the season, Tim, one of the lead boatmen, and Fred were in the restaurant talking about who they were going to hire next year, and I was just kind of standing by eavesdropping. I could hear Tim say, 'Well, we still have to hire a swamper.' And Fred said, 'No, we've got a swamper,' and Tim said, 'Yeah, that's right.' And I'm thinking, shit. . . .

“Well, I finally got enough nerve to walk in and say, ‘Who’s the swamper going to be?’

“They looked up and said, ‘You are.’ And Fred said, ‘But don’t think for one minute I’m ever going to let you be a boatman.’

“And I said, ‘Fred, I’m not going to be a swamper unless you’re going to let me be a boatman.’

“And Fred said, ‘Well, I ain’t going to have a girl driving a boat down there.’

“Fred was really a great guy, but he’d made up his mind, and I’d made up my mind. We both laid it on the table.

“The boatmen who were running that next year took really good care of me and taught me how to drive a boat. I’m a very conservative boatman. I don’t hang it out there. I tried to be really careful because I was really scared of hurting someone.” Connie said she was fortunate to learn to drive motor rigs during low-water years when it was extremely challenging to run a motor rig. The “old boys” also taught her that when the going got rough in a rapid, to forget looking good and just sit down, brace herself, and hang on to the motor.

“I worked as hard as I could for them, and they stood up for me at the end. By the end of the summer, Fred needed a fifth boatman. The boatmen told him, ‘Fred, you’ve got a fifth boatman.’ ” As Connie said, it was history from there. As to exactly what date in history, she, like most of the boatwomen, isn’t really quite sure. “I have a T-shirt that came out of that era that says winter 76–77, so I bet I swamped in 1976 and was running in 1977.”

Connie didn’t sit around and wonder what to do during the off-season. Every winter she took her money and went to a drop zone somewhere to sky-dive and buy ratings: commercial pilot, multi-engine, and instrument. She worked on planes, too, to earn her mechanic's license. During the river season, there were a couple of years where she did most of the maintenance on the motors. "I'm a natural wrench. I get along fine with machinery. Don't get me wrong—it's not a love for mechanics; it's something I can do. It's not really that fun working with my arm up to my elbow in a bucket of oil."

When I met Connie at her house high in the cliffs near Marble Canyon, she was working on one of her four vehicles. As she drove us back down the dirt road to pick up her truck at the Ferry, I glanced out the window. The view of the plateau was spectacular. Off in the distance was the dark slit where the Colorado starts seriously sculpturing the Grand Canyon. On the drive up to Connie's house, I had avoided looking out at the empty space only one foot from the steep road. It was a drop-off only a parachutist could love.

"I never pay more than $300 for a car," Connie said. I asked her if she ever got nervous on this road. "Yeah, a couple of times when there were no brakes on my half-ton."

Connie began to enjoy flying planes as much as jumping out of them. In 1982, she was washing an airplane when a pilot walked up to her and asked if she wanted a soda pop. "I hate soda pop. I never drink soda pop, but I said, 'Yeah.' " Turns out this man, whom she referred to as "God's best," needed a copilot. They ended up flying around together for a few years, delivering planes to folks in exotic parts of the world. "We didn't work cheap, and we'd go places where other people wouldn't go."

Now, for part of the year, Connie works as a flight engineer on a DC-6 up in Alaska, and this winter, she is flying between Chile and Antarctica. "I want to be the pilot, but first you have to work as an engineer to get to know the plane.

“It’s not like flying jets where you have to wear shiny shoes and be presentable. It’s an airline with the same standards as American and United, but you go to work in blue jeans, handle freight, and deal with problems that come up. They pretty much give you enough training so that if something goes wrong with the airplane, they expect you to bring it home.

“I like the old airplanes, and the people in the business are somewhat like boatmen. They’re there because they like it. Although, they’re cool: they don’t hug each other, and even though they rely on each other, they don’t admit it.

“There’s nobody like boatmen. It’s the most supportive environment I’ve ever been in. When you’re down there with a crew that you’re getting along with, man, you can’t get life any better than that. Now I’m getting into a colder world, but I think I’m strong enough to handle it—if I can just keep remembering where the strength comes from, which is pretty much in The Ditch, the Canyon.”

Even when she was delivering planes, she always managed a few trips in the Canyon. “We were a really fun, tight group,” Connie said. “And at ARR we got to know all the other guides, because everyone stopped in at Vermilion Cliffs. It felt like we were the center of the universe.” Eventually, Fred Burke sold his river company. Now Connie works eight-day trips for Grand Canyon Expeditions and freelances for other motor companies. “Last year, I ran for everybody. I like freelancing. It’s harder because you’re never on top of the equipment or menu, but you get to know different people and equipment. And there are places in the Canyon where certain companies stop all the time, or things some people know about that nobody else does.

“Last year was the first full season I’ve run in awhile. Every year, it has been a real bitter decision. What should I do? What should I do? I keep trying to be practical and say, you've got to do something to plan for your future."

I asked her why she kept coming back—was it the River or the Canyon? "I don't separate the two; it's just a good place." She talked about special places down there: the rich red Supai formation in Marble Canyon; the pink granite intrusions in the Inner Gorge; the sculptured pot holes around Mile 212; the rapids.

"That stupid Canyon," she said. "If it wasn't for that place, I'd be a millionaire."

CHAPTER 11

Sue Bennett

Sue Bassett

"Oh god," said Sue Bassett. "I have to introduce myself and get to know these people? I think I'm going to throw up.

"I'd be really freaked out at the put-in. I didn't like it when the bus came. I'd go hide in the bushes sometimes. My stomach would be in knots. But as soon as I pushed off from Lee's Ferry, it was unbelievable. It was so consistent, I knew I could count on it. There was this peace of mind, and that's the first thing that comes up remembering the river—peace of mind.

"I probably feel more at home down there than any place in my entire life, completely comfortable, like I belong."

Sue B, as everyone calls her, came to the Grand Canyon from about as far away as you can get—New York City. No matter how rumpled or dirty Sue B is, she always has an air of eastern sophistication, a certain poise. With her thick, light brown hair, large blue-gray eyes, and tall, thin physique, she carries a natural elegance. However, that attribute may not have been apparent back when she was a kid. "I was on the milk and crackers list for years at camp. You know, if you were skinny you had to stop playing midmorning to eat a snack. They almost didn't let me take lifesaving because they didn't think I was up to it."

I asked her what she had dreamed of doing when she grew

up. "I was going to be a horse," she said. But Sue B ended up following more traditional pursuits, sort of. She quit college after her third year. "I thought a bolt of lightning was going to knock me dead because in 1963 you did not quit college." Her parents were supportive, as always, but a month after she quit, her mom woke her up and said, "Get up, I've called Hickox Secretarial School. They're expecting you in an hour." Sue B said she had "no retort, no alternative, so I went."

After about nine years of working as a secretary, first in Boston and then in New York City, Sue B was going a little crazy. "I worked for Marcel Breuer, whose designer furniture is now in art museums. I thought I was having a mental breakdown—all this blatant consumerism and preoccupation with image. I didn't know that there was any other way to be. I didn't blend in. I was the only one in New York on the bus heading to the recycling center with my bag of recyclables. And then, when I was twenty-seven years old, I went on this river trip and met people who thought like me."

Sue B first heard about Grand Canyon river trips from two acquaintances who had been at a convention in Texas. While there they decided, well, we're this close, let's go see the Grand Canyon. "I mean," Sue B said, "how provincial can you get? They had no idea how far away they were from the Grand Canyon."

While her friends stood looking over the Canyon rim, they met someone fresh off a river trip. It sounded like great fun, so when they returned to New York, one of them convinced Sue B that they should go down the river together. "I didn't really want to go on an organized group trip. I hate groups."

The outfitter Sue B eventually signed up with in 1972 was ARTA. "I remember meeting some of the passengers at a pretrip meeting and thinking, god, if they're on my trip, I'm going to die. They seemed so nerdy. Of course, they were the greatest people in the world. We still correspond. And I'd expected the boatmen to be cowboys with pieces of hay in their teeth. Instead, they were from Dartmouth and Yale, an extraordinary group."

So at twenty-seven years old, it was downriver from there. Sue B came out west and learned to row in the ARTA Whitewater School, which traveled around to various rivers. Actually, her going to the school was a boatman's suggestion. He also told her that California was "where all the women worked." But Sue B really wasn't thinking about being a "boatman"; she just wanted to get back on the river. "I was very nervous, but the first person I met at the whitewater school was female. And Peter Winn was the director. I remembered seeing Peter at the end of my first Canyon trip as we were motoring the row boats out across the lake to take-out. He put on twenty life jackets and was floating ten feet above the surface of Lake Mead, just a big ball, all you could see were his arms and legs.

"Peter set the tone for the whitewater school so well. His attitude was such that he never made women feel that they couldn't do it or would have to work harder. I remember him saying, 'I know a woman can row the Grand Canyon. I know it.'

"At the school, it seemed that everything I had ever known became totally invalid. None of the ploys I would unwittingly use in New York to impress people worked out in the middle of nowhere. Any sophisticated cynicism and snobbery backfired, and I became the fool. The river was such an equalizer. Facades fell away as we realized the mutual need for one another."

After the whitewater school, Sue B worked rivers in California for ARTA, although she still considered guiding a temporary break before she found a "nice job." In 1975, she helped to teach the whitewater school. "I learned more about rowing that year than any other time. Afterwards, I rowed a couple of Middle Fork trips in Idaho, and it was like I was sitting behind myself, talking to myself. I could hear my own voice in my ear as an instructor. I could just see the river like an X-ray. It was the most control I've ever felt in my whole life."

After a long drought and the resulting shortage of river work in California, Sue B was offered a job in Idaho with Wilderness World. This outfit was owned by an eccentric Czechoslovakian named Vladimir, who, rumor had it, had once escaped from a prison train heading for Siberia. He had never hired a woman to row in Idaho (or in the Grand Canyon, where he also had a permit). Sue B said, "He actually had boatmen in California who would have killed to go up to Idaho, but I already had an Idaho river license, so it was less hassle. Plus Vladimir thought he was desperate."

One reason California guides wanted to work in Idaho (other than its beauty) was that trips were longer, usually one week instead of weekends. And the pay was much better: $60 per day, instead of $25, even more than some Grand Canyon boatmen were making back then.

In 1977, at the end of the Idaho season, Sue B came down to the Grand Canyon to row a baggage boat for Wilderness World. One of the crew told her, "I've never seen a woman who can row, but you can row." She stayed in the Canyon, but it took awhile before Sue B stopped missing the technical water up north. "Lots of people would get nervous at Upset Rapid at low water, but I'd be thinking, 'Oh boy, rocks! Let's see if I can miss this one by half an inch.' "

Sue B was a rare guide in that she loved Horn Creek Rapid at very low water. At higher levels, the two black rocks at the top, the horns, are buried. But not at low water. Nothing is buried. It is all exposed and noisy. Years ago, the first time our crew stood on the slick black rocks of the Inner Gorge to scout low-water Horn, even the most macho of our boatmen looked slightly sick. We watched a motor boat's tube explode when it slammed into the razor edge of the black protruding cliff near the end of this rocky rapid. Horn Creek is full of other goodies, too: steep waterfall-like pour-overs and big waves, obstacles that make it hard to miss the sharp wall waiting for you at the bottom.

Sue B was terrified on her first run, but learned, "You could do beautiful runs if you floated through in the right spot. What people would do is they'd be nervous and want to stay away from the center and the big hole at the bottom. They'd pull right and hit the rocks near shore and actually have to turn around and row out, but they'd hit that big jagged rock at the bottom.

"But you hung out there, you hung out there, a little farther out than you'd ever think you'd want to be. And it took a lot of self-control because you're thinking, 'I want to get to the right side, why am I out here?'

"Have faith. Okay, down you go into these huge waves and you're thinking, 'I know when I get to the other side of this wave I'm going into that hole, and I'm going to die.' But what it did," Sue B said, gesturing gracefully with her long hand, "is slide you off so you didn't even take a stroke through the whole rapid. It was really amazing. But you had to be out there."

Sue B could show a really calm face above rapids, no matter how she felt inside. She may have learned that trick back when she was six years old, back when she would pretend to be an Indian. "We'd arrive at my gram's summer camp, and

I'd go right to the costume chest, get the Indian jacket out, and wear it the whole week. It had two little arrows and fringe. I'd absolutely practice really hard to not show any emotion because I thought that's what Indians did. I would not smile."

Quite a few of the early Canyon boatwomen felt intense pressure not to screw up in rapids. Sue B was no exception. "It was a private thing that no one knew about but me. I just felt really obligated. I knew there weren't that many women down there, and if there were going to be more, I wanted to set a little groundwork.

"But I'll tell you, working for ARTA in California, especially with Peter Winn, made all the difference in my switching over to Wilderness World, because I had no chip on my shoulder. I didn't feel it was strange for a woman to run rivers, so I didn't feel defensive. I'd seen so many women trying to break into rowing with Wilderness World, and I hate to say this, but I saw this defensiveness more often than not. And I saw women whine and whimper and ask for help a lot. One baggage boatwoman asked for assistance rowing in the wind. I hold very high standards, and that means my hands would bleed before I'd ask for help. Just to get it clear, just to let them know I could do it.

"And I have to admit that in the beginning I would lift things that were absurd, like pressing bulky two-hundred-pound rafts over the side of the truck. We all did. But, after five years on the river and enough boatmen hurting their backs, it became clear that it was stupid."

Back when few women ran the Colorado commercially, watching passengers' reactions was a treat. As Sue B said, "People reassessed their own roles as they watched me do exceedingly strenuous work or watched the total ease with which the male members of the crew and I related to one another. When it came to doing heavy work on the trips, such as everyone shoving stranded boats offshore after the water dropped, invariably men would quickly volunteer to help and women would stand and watch. I remember one frustrated boatman yelling at the women passengers, 'What do you think, your arms are painted on?' "

Wilderness World was a small company, so Sue B pretty much worked with the same seven-man crew for six years, averaging ten trips a year with only four or five days in between. (In a larger company, crew composition changes, and there can be more time off between trips.) I asked her if her schedule got tiring. She said, basically, no. "It was heaven being with those guys. They were superlative." She thought her schedule looked mellow compared to a few other companies where they never got a day off. "Those guys had to be demented."

Like all guides, Sue B had her special places in the Canyon. "My favorite place in the whole Canyon is Shinumo Amphitheater. We would get pounded by big water in the [Inner] Gorge, and then the amphitheater was like these arms, this opening up of the cliffs, that said, 'Welcome.'

"And there are the secret places down there that I never shared with anybody, that I went to by myself."

Sue B had some strong reasons for leaving the Canyon in 1982 and walking away from her ten-year career running rivers. "It was a combination of things, but mainly, I didn't really like my attitude down there. It was a double-edged sword. On the one hand, people were telling me how wonderful I was, and I knew damn well I was just a normal person. I could count on one hand, maybe, the passengers who talked to me as an equal, not this incredible boatwoman.

"I'd tell the people, 'Well, the guys are just as wonderful. They work just as hard, they get just as tired and just as scared. I mean, I've seen those guys with their knees knocking. Don't single me out.' I just kept wanting to get people to see us all as people.

"But on the other hand, I reveled in it. I'd tell them it would be really nice if someday there's other women down here and nobody notices that I'm unique. But I also thought, it's going to be kind of sad, because I love being the only one here."

She was the only woman at Wilderness World until Debi Hendrick began training in 1980. But the glory of being on a pedestal can wear thin, so Sue B chose to leave.

"I suddenly felt like I was down in a hole in the ground. The whole world was passing by up on the rim, and I was getting out of touch. I was going to have to make a choice—to stay on the river and put all my eggs in one basket or to get back in touch and be functional again in a normal society.

"I was also getting a little cynical about changing the world. That was one of our missions. It astounded me how ignorant people were about environmental issues, like where their water came from. I gave myself the role of the educator, mostly by example. Seems to me the most effect I've ever had, or the effect I'm most pleased with, is when I didn't say anything, but I set an example that somebody noticed. The river was a wonderful vehicle for that. But if somebody wanted to hear about it, believe me, they heard about it. I tried to get them in tears when we went by the Marble Canyon dam site. [In the mid-1960s, the upper Grand Canyon came close to being dammed at this site.] If I just got one person to turn their water off while they brushed their teeth, I guess I've been a success.

"But I didn't like my feeling of superiority. I knew it was hogwash, but I couldn't seem to stop it. Looking down on people was a really easy trap to fall into, because you're on your turf and they're not.

"It was very humbling when I started doing menial stuff for

the photographers John Running and Sue Bennett in Flagstaff. People would ask, 'What do you do?' Instead of answering, 'I work on the river,' and hearing a typical reaction like, 'Really? Wow!,' now when I said, 'I'm a photographer's assistant,' I heard a flat reaction like, 'Oh . . .' I loved it! It was comforting and the biggest high after I got used to it, to be an average person, to not be special."

Sue B still works for Running and Bennett. And over the years, by saving and doing most of the work herself, she built a stunning, self-sufficient adobe home in the piñon and juniper forest outside of town.

Sue B laughed when she talked about a test she took from her uncle, who was chairman of the board of a lumber company. The test was used to assess an employee's potential and personality. "My test showed that I was persistent and determined, but that I didn't like people.

" 'But, Uncle Bob,' I said, 'I like people.'

"He replied, 'Well, of course you do. Everybody likes people, but I mean *really* like people.' And I started realizing that I was not a public person. I was a very formal, private person. It was an effort all those years on the river to be as open as I was. I kept people at a distance as a protection; they wanted to know everything. They would ask me the most incredibly personal questions—like about my love life. I mean, would you have the gall to ask someone you didn't even know about their love life? I like people very much, but not enough to give them my entire soul. I felt like I just got sucked dry. I ran out of steam. I didn't have any more.

"I miss the camaraderie of the crew, the 'pards,' as we called them. I miss the river, but it was such a luxury, and I knew it was at the time. I always thought that even if I have to scrub floors for the rest of my life, it will be all right, because I did this."

CHAPTER 12

Lorna Corson

David Edwards. Color slide.

Lorna Corson looks like the classic surfer girl: she is a petite blond with well-defined muscles who walks barefoot as much as possible. Lorna is as quiet and smooth as the morning sea, but it is not the ocean you will see reflected in her clear blue eyes; it is the solid rock of the mountains of Wyoming or the smooth slickrock of Southwestern deserts. Although she briefly considered the career possibilities of trapeze walking, dancing, or working as an architect, in 1972 she enrolled as a geology student at Northern Arizona University in Flagstaff. "It was the only major that made any sense; I could be outside more."

"I did a lot of hiking in the Canyon on the Tonto Plateau, a borderline trail then. I spent days just staring at the river, but I didn't really think of running it. Then I started running the Salt River on weekends with some geology friends who were always talking about the Colorado. I knew then that I would go down, that I had to."

One day Lorna packed her sleeping bag in a small backpack and hitchhiked across the Navajo Reservation up to Lee's Ferry. "I asked boatmen at the Ferry if they needed any help, and finally this motor boatman said, yeah, I could go on a trip. His intentions weren't clear, but he looked harmless enough, and I figured I could straighten that out later. But then his boss got onto it and said I couldn't come, so the boatman told me to meet him downstream at Phantom." (Phantom Ranch consists of several cabins for rent, a primitive campground, mule corrals, a dining room, and a ranger station. Nestled under cottonwoods along Bright Angel Creek, Phantom is the popular destination for hikers and for the famous Canyon mule-train ride.)

Leaving Lee's Ferry, Lorna hitchhiked up to the cool pines of the North Rim, and then walked down into the heat of the inner Canyon, following a thirteen-mile trail that drops 5,800 feet to Phantom Ranch. "I was at Phantom a day early and decided to go meet him upriver at Clear Creek." So that same day she hiked nine more miles over the hot waterless trail that traverses the plateau on top of the Inner Gorge, a thousand feet above the river. "It was May, and I had one quart of water. It was one of the stupidest things I've done. I ran out of water and got really dehydrated. I started to almost hallucinate, thinking there were rattlesnakes everywhere. Finally, I got down to Clear Creek and just threw myself in and drank until my stomach was fully distended. I hiked on down the creek and slept on a little island because I was worried about snakes. I just had a tiny backpack, no ground cloth, no pad.

"The next day, I made it to the river and hailed the first boat I saw, a motor boat. I found out that the fellow I was supposed to meet had already passed. I told the motor guides, a couple, that I didn't think I should walk back to Phantom with just a quart of water. They said, 'Hop on! You might as well come with us as far as Havasu.'" So she did, hiked out and hitchhiked back home to Flagstaff via old Route 66.

That was 1976. The river experience had captivated her. "I considered hanging around trying to get on trips but went up to Washington instead. I worked in the northern Cascades for a geologist studying the contact of a granite batholith to see if it would be worth mining the copper. My conscience couldn't handle it, and I got really homesick for Arizona."

Lorna returned to Flagstaff, and as fate would have it, fell in love with an AZRA boatman, which led to a few more Canyon trips. By 1978, she was working for AZRA.

"I was determined and ready to have my own boat. It was a great relief to find a niche in society. My dad was a Park Service ranger. I had a beautiful, isolated childhood. My three sisters and younger brother and I lived in really remote places early on. In Alaska we hardly saw anyone for two years; we had no exposure to the outside world. When we saw people, we were all really shy kids."

Lorna worried that she was too quiet and shy to work as a river guide. On her early trips, a few passengers asked the other boatmen, "Does Lorna ever talk?" While it is true that she is more low-key than most other AZRA boatwomen, and it may seem that she doesn't say much, that is only if you are more than two feet away from her soft voice. It is well worth it to be within range of her cryptic wit. She may use words sparingly, but it would be a mistake to assume that she doesn't have an extensive use of the English language. I remember one passenger, who had written a thesaurus, strutting up the beach to play Scrabble with the guides. He came back muttering to himself, dismayed that Lorna had slaughtered him at the game.

Although she's not a performer ("I hate public speaking"), she enjoys conversations. Certain passengers always flock to her boat. Her quiet qualities are appreciated by the other boatmen as well. "It's a treat to do a trip with Lorna," one fellow guide said. "There's a real strength and consistency with her that you don't always find. Lorna doesn't depend on any props at all. It's like her boat. There's nothing extra in there. She keeps it clean, she keeps it simple. There's an incredible beauty to that."

Lorna also keeps stashes of various health foods stuffed in the ammo boxes on her boat: nuts, tahini, and the like. A strict vegetarian, she's extremely conscious about what foods she puts in her body and about keeping fit, though pretty near every activity she enjoys easily keeps her in shape.

"On my first trips, I rowed as much flatwater as anyone would let me. I knew as soon as I started rowing that I wanted to row. I loved rowing."

At five foot, three inches, Lorna's heard a lot of teasing about being short, things like "too short to reach the pedals." She's pretty much had it ("up to here") with short jokes. In the beginning of her career, she just piled a bunch of stuff in front of her feet to brace against. Actually, she did worry a bit that she might not get hired because of her size, but when she met me she had hope "because you were so scrawny. Plus, I noticed that you and Jessie were afraid above some of the rapids. At that time I was never afraid."

Yet it wasn't the rapids that drew Lorna to the Canyon—it was the landscape. "I like Marble Canyon because the rock is so much purer; downriver it's more jumbled. And the Nankoweap area, I can still feel the ancient Indians who lived there. If you wanted to live down there, that would be the obvious place. The Colorado's most aesthetic to me when it's emerald clear, but I'm transfixed on the landscape more than the river. I like the upper Canyon easily as much as the river corridor. And I like the heat very much, the intensity of it. The river's beautiful and a great way to travel, but it's not for the whitewater thrills that I go down there at all. I go down there to be in the Canyon, to be away from the real world."

Ah yes, the real world . . . and what to do when it is time to go back at the end of the river season? What can follow days illuminated with the Canyon's magical, salmon-pink light? It is very hard to come back to the top where people are running around doing all kinds of crazy things to each other. As Lorna said, "We bond so quickly down there; you make friends like never seems to happen anywhere else." After the season, Lorna still manages to get as far away as she can from the real world. She winters in a small snowy Wyoming town.

The first thing she used to do after working full seasons was rest. Although river guiding is fun, it is emotionally and physically exhausting. "I just get wired and stay wired until the trip's over," Lorna said. After a trip, many guides can do little but sleep for a few days. Even someone in Lorna's excellent shape is just plain tired after a season working in the Canyon's heat. But after an initial rest period, winter was, as Lorna described it, "the annual crisis, wondering what you're going to do and what you're worth. You go from thinking you're the hottest thing on earth to nothing. Not being part of a community. People don't take you seriously. And always the next river season takes precedence over commitments.

"I found it nearly impossible to work full seasons and have a real relationship. But for nine years, I decided it was worth it." Then, one Wyoming winter, Lorna met a carpenter and climbing guide named Norm, and she decided it wasn't worth it anymore. "But I can't picture myself just not coming back to the river. I cut back to half-seasons because I found my life a bit schizophrenic—The Canyon and The Other Life—and hoped to integrate it a little more. But I miss not seeing my buddies enough, and I find it hard to be less important in the company.

"But there is a lot of northern country to see that is only accessible in summer." Even though Lorna loves the mountains, she needs to come back to the Canyon every year—to laugh with her river pals and to converse with passengers from different walks of life. And she comes back to feel the pleasure of rowing. "I love rowing more than anything, except skiing perfect powder. Rowing's in my cells now. Every spring I think about the river. Just like every fall I start to think about ski season."

Lorna rows gracefully and likes being in control. Her least-favorite rapid is unpredictable Granite. "It's sloppy, there's no finesse." Lorna's favorite rapid is Deubendorff at low water, when you have to make an exact entry or risk smashing into black fang rocks disguised as foam at the bottom. "I love reading the water, estimating what you think it will do, getting your angles right, and finding out how close your calculations were—just the physics of water."

However, some precise entries aren't her favorite, such as Crystal during the high-water years. "Crystal definitely took away any cockiness I had. We'd all seen it enough at high water that year to know what ugly meant, and heard all the horror stories too, like, 'They flipped three out of three last time . . .' One day in 1983, we got to Crystal, and it was awful looking. Nobody felt like running it. I don't know what was different about it that day, but it was early on during the high water so we hadn't run it much. It just looked like we were all going to die. The huge laterals fed into the flip wave, and if that didn't get you, the next hole would. There were about a hundred people there, like there used to be when all the trips stopped to deal with high-water Crystal. There'd been a lot of boats flipping that day and the day before. After scouting, the head boatman announced, 'We'll line the boats.' A private trip had just portaged, and OU [Outdoors Unlimited] was considering it. We'd never done that, and we had a rather weak crew, only four of us and a lot of elderly passengers.

"Lining is really dangerous, I think." The idea of lining is to move the unloaded rafts past the worst part of the rapid by controlling them from shore with ropes. "There was kind of a channel on the right and a pour-over rock at the top where the wave came off that was feeding right out into the hole. We tried to bring the boats inside that pour-over by lining them in the slow water and lifting them over the rocks. The boatmen were in the water, and the passengers held ropes from upstream slowing the boats down. People who could hardly walk on rocks anyway were trying to hold onto a two-ton boat from that boulder-strewn shoreline. Luckily an OU boatman helped us. Having that one extra person made a difference. We had de-rigged the boats some, carried some of the heavy gear around.

"This whole process took hours—ropes, tension, confusion, and noise. After two boats, we broke for lunch. Then OU successfully rowed their big [twelve-foot] raft through. One of our boatmen decided he would try and row his boat through. My boat and his were the only ones left to line. 'What are you going to do?' he asked me at lunch. 'Puke, first off,' I said.

"He ran his and had an exquisite run inside the pour-over rock. Okay, I decided, I can do that too. I'd run right over that rock, crunch right over it. But if I wasn't near or on that rock, or lost my oars, or got out of control there, I wasn't going to make it.

"Entering the tongue of that ugly, angry rapid, I could not have been further right. There were a hundred witnesses and photographers.

"So there I was rowing backward over the pour-over, both oars flying up and out. I was airborne trying not to let them go. The propane bottle under the load kicked on, hissing. My first impulse after assessing my oarless situation was, wouldn't it be just sensational to light a match as I dive into Crystal, a flaming raft right down the center of the rapid? But instead, I managed to get one oar in as I entered the second hole, got the second oar back in time for the island hole, and pulled the two-thousand-pound pig into the Alive Below Crystal eddy. Covered with oarlock grease and lucky again! I popped a beer and remembered why we do this. Three weeks till I'm at the top again!

"But it was no joke. I remember running it for those three high-water years, getting nervous a couple of days before. We'd end up spending a whole day there every trip. I had so many pinball runs there."

It has been said that because women weren't as strong, they had to be more cunning. "I remember I got behind Lorna and just followed her," one tall, lanky boatman said. "I was amazed at how effortlessly she rowed the boat—very quietly, just the way she is. And I started realizing this woman could really read water, so I started paying attention to her runs and what she was doing.

"One time, I'd just come through Deubendorff. It was a pretty exciting [water] level, real technical, big ledges and holes. I pulled into the beach at the bottom and looked back up at the rapid. Just then, a big motor boat came through with people yelling and screaming. They pulled in next to us with a boat full of these big, big guys, like a football team or something. They were drunk and obnoxious, yelling and screaming, looking at our boats and making comments.

"One of them yelled, 'Here comes another boat!' And another yelled, 'It's a woman!' They ran up the beach to watch, and they started yelling, 'Oh man, I bet she's some big kinda Amazon woman, a macho woman. Just our type.' And they got real excited. 'Here's a wooooman. She's probably got huge bazoogas and can reeeeally pull those oars.' They were just ranting and raving.

"And here comes ol' Lorna, you know, just as quiet and peaceful as she could be. She just has this nice run and very easily pulls her boat into the eddy and gets out. And those guys looked at her in all her quiet splendor and they were silent. They were dumbfounded. They humbly went and climbed back on their boat."

Lorna may not yell and scream at the bottom of rapids, but her eyes are shouting. There's more than a little macho spirit in her. Her sister Annie said they could always entice her to climb anything by saying, "I bet you can't do this." Lorna is still climbing, but with ropes since she met Norm. She breaks out in hives in a crowded city but looks pretty calm making a crucial move up some sheer wall.

"I love the gymnastics of it, also the improbable places you can get to—mostly getting further up a canyon to see what's up there. When I began climbing with ropes, my fear of exposure was great, despite the fact that some climbing I'd done in the Canyon unroped was more dangerous. It took a couple of years to at least get my fears more rational, because it's no more dangerous a thousand feet up than fifty. I'm into the adrenaline of it, but I'm more into making difficult moves over rock. And the airiness does make being on the ground a bit mundane after awhile."

Lorna admits she prefers climbing on warm summer days. "I have to force myself to go mountaineering; fighting the cold and worrying about avalanche or icefall isn't my idea of a good time." Still, she will be a good wife and go ice climbing with her husband now and then. "I've had some very pleasant mountaineering days. For instance, Norm and I climbed one mountain in Nepal when it was a clear, sunny day, a small ice pitch, mixed rock and snow, and a hairline ridge to the summit. I do like altitude, it does wild things; but I don't like what mountaineers call objective dangers, things you have no control over."

Lorna has recently worked as a carpenter and drafter, and although she hasn't found her perfect second career yet, she's figured out how to enjoy life. A good part of her time is spent outdoors with Norm doing what she loves: running, hiking, climbing, and skiing. And when spring comes, it is back to the Canyon and the river. After all, it's in her cells.

CHAPTER 13

A Real Boat

When Huck Finn pushed off into the Mississippi, he waxed poetic about his homemade raft: "We said there warn't no home like a raft, after all. Other places do seem so cramped up and smothery, but a raft don't. You feel mighty free and easy and comfortable on a raft."[1]

For many river guides, being on an inflatable raft is exactly like that. It is home. But to the boatmen and women at Grand Canyon Dories, an inflatable raft isn't even considered a boat. And they have their reasons for that—good ones.

To these river guides, a colorfully painted, eighteen-foot wooden dory equipped with storage hatches is a boat, and a rubber raft . . . well, a raft is something you train on, something you row until you can row your own dory. As one dory boatwoman said, "I can remember people saying it's a five-boat trip or a six-boat trip, but they never even counted the inflatable baggage raft that was along. Not only didn't they ever count us, but you would never want the raft in any pictures."

If you didn't have eyes, you might think this was snobbery,

1. Mark Twain, *The Adventures of Huckleberry Finn*, large-type edition (New York: Grolier, 1955), p. 129.

but all you need to do is see a dory on the water to realize it is pure aesthetics. Dories are, without a doubt, the most beautiful crafts on the Colorado. And they handle as beautifully as they look.

"Oh, I couldn't believe getting off the inflatable baggage raft," a dory boatwoman said. "The raft had forty-two bags tied on, with chains holding the floor. It was noisy, it buckled. My hands were raw from tying in bags night and day. And then I got onto a *boat*, a dory. The first thing that amazed me was how quiet a dory was. I mean, they just slide over the waves; they just break through the water. Nothing's rattling, nothing's flopping, nothing's squishing, or squeezing, or pinching.

"The way a dory handles is like night and day compared to a raft. Oh, a dory's just so responsive—it breaks the water so beautifully, it pivots so fast, it glides. I mean, you can track in the water and not lose momentum in the wind. But mostly, it's the way a dory feels over waves—instead of just sploshing through them, a dory slices through waves. It feels everything, so it's responding to every up and down. They are just such a joy to row."

There is a down side to the dories. Because of their narrow six-foot beam, they do flip easier than a raft. And if they hit a rock, they tend to crunch. Dory boatmen sometimes scout rapids through binoculars to see the precise shape of waves and to look for chine diggers, rocks just below the surface. If the water is too low, the trip waits until the river rises, which happens daily because of the dam's fluctuating water releases. "Sometimes we see all these rubber rafts go through the rapid and they're having a great time and you think, yeah, that makes sense," said one dory guide. Dory boatmen also constantly worry about where to park in order to prevent their wooden boats from grinding into rocks as the water surges or the river level fluctuates.

But to the dory boatmen and women, these are small prices to pay for rowing a graceful, highly maneuverable boat that literally dances on the water.

Martin Litton designed these particular dories back in the early 1960s and then created a company called Grand Canyon Dories, which offered eighteen- to twenty-day trips all the way to Lake Mead. (One of Martin's first guides always said that he rowed through the Grand Canyon for free but got paid $500 to row across Lake Mead.) Martin was instrumental in stopping a proposed Marble Canyon dam in the 1960s. Each of his brightly painted dories was named for a beautiful place that had been destroyed by humans and lost to us, names such as "Stanislaus," "Tapestry Wall," "Music Temple," "Makaha." Martin could be pretty crusty, but his boatmen loved him, even though, as one boatman put it, "Martin always thought we should be paying him for the privilege of rowing his boats." And he also made no secret of his opinions regarding women rowing dories. They should be in the kitchen and in the boatmen's . . . well, they were in the kitchen for quite awhile.

In 1987, Martin Litton sold his company. Luckily, one of the buyers, George Wendt of OARS, decided to keep running these beautiful boats in addition to OARS' rubber rafts.

Rubber rafts, unless they need patching, lie rolled up and forgotten in the warehouse waiting for the next trip. In contrast, dory boatmen often spent hours sanding and painting their boats when they worked for Martin in the old warehouse up in Hurricane, Utah. One guide said, "We felt so connected to our boats. We sort of turned them into these art objects. Each little boat had its history." After George Wendt bought the dories, a few guides spent two winters fiberglassing the boats. "Martin would never fiberglass the boats," one boatwoman said. "We talked George into stripping, repainting, and glassing them. They didn't get any heavier because all the old paint that came off equaled the weight of the glass that went on. It was like history chipping those layers of paint off."

History and love. For the dory guides, it is not just a love affair with the Grand Canyon. It is also a love affair with a brightly painted boat. "They're so pretty," said Ellen Tibbetts, who has rowed dories for many years. "They're completely different than anything else. Well, they're boats. I think that's the difference. They're actually boats."

CHAPTER 14

Ellen Tibbetts

Raechel M. Running

Ellen Tibbetts[1] worked almost seven years for Martin Litton cooking and rowing a baggage raft before she rowed her first wooden dory filled with commercial passengers through the Grand Canyon. But Ellen is quick to say that it wasn't Martin's fault that it took so long. "It had a lot more to do with my own feelings than anything else stopping me. Even though Martin would joke, I always felt supported."

Ellen, a ceramic artist, is very quiet and unassuming. While we talked, I could feel her mind racing through her thoughts. Yet she speaks slowly and chooses her words carefully, as if she is trying to find the perfect shape for a piece of clay out of all the many possibilities. Ellen is five feet four inches tall with long, straight blond hair, big, steady, beautiful blue eyes, and long eyelashes set under delicately arched brows. Poised, slow, and graceful, there is a certain gentle calm about her, but it is easy to sense the fire underneath—she's more like an ember than a flame. Ellen admits that she's not outgoing. You might not pick her out of a crowd as an adventurer or river guide, but as usual, looks can be deceiving.

"If I was going to talk about memorable trips," Ellen said

1. Ellen is not related to Connie Tibbetts.

quietly, "the one I would have to tell about was in 1983 when we left on 60,000 cfs and it kept coming up and coming up. The place that took us all by surprise was Deer Creek Narrows. We had just come through Helicopter Eddy, and all of a sudden we were fighting for our lives, trying to stay off the walls, trying to not hit each other. It was crazy. And then within minutes, we were at Deer Creek Falls [where a seventy-foot waterfall tumbles out from a cleft in the brown sandstone]. It was even hard to row into Deer Creek. We had to pull and pull and pull, and when we were tired of pulling, we had to keep pulling. People who had already landed would run along shore and throw lines to the boats coming in.

"I remember if I saw somebody pulling in way downstream, I'd think, okay, I'd better get ready. I don't know why they're pulling in, but I'd better make it. I just figured I'd power in and hope for the best, and hope that any upwelling boils would boil me in instead of out of the eddy.

"After we ran Crystal that trip, we camped at Bass [ten miles below Crystal], which was an incredibly hard place to pull in. I missed it, but I got into an eddy below and lined my boat up along the cliff far enough to where I could unload all the people and food. Then I let my boat back down and tied up below, climbed over the cliff, and got back to camp.

"The next morning as we were breaking the kitchen down and loading things up, a motor boat floated by upside down. It had flipped in Crystal. The people riding on top of it were completely freaked out, holding up 'Need Help' throw cushions and screaming, saying they didn't know where everybody was. We got out there as fast as we could.

"The motor rig broached and stuck on that corner at Mile 110 and a couple of our boats pulled in there. Everybody was eventually accounted for. A couple of people were hurt.

We went downstream and helped them radio a helicopter. The next day we saw a couple more boats come floating by upside down.

"When we were at Havasu, the Park Service dropped us a note saying that the river was coming up to 92,000 [cfs]. That volume of water was so different—the most power I've ever felt in my life—and we were on it. If it ever happens again, I will do it again in a second."

Ellen grew up in Wisconsin, and when it was time to choose a college, she picked Northern Arizona University. ("I don't remember why exactly; I just wanted to go out west.") She first saw the Grand Canyon in 1969 after she joined the hiking club at school. At the club's first meeting, someone announced that the president and vice-president of the club were lost somewhere in the Grand Canyon. [It was, in fact, Sue Billingsley's Mohawk Canyon hiking group.] Ellen thought, "Great! This is the club for me!" She emphasized that "they weren't really lost, they were missing. They knew where they were. I didn't think they were in danger or anything. I just thought they were out there somewhere in the middle of nowhere and that would be the thing that I would want to do."

She spent the next five years hiking in the Canyon. "There was a main core of us. School was great, but what we really lived for was going out on weekends to have these adventures. The core group evolved over the years. Each year the club started out with maybe thirty people, but after the first 'easy' hike down somewhere like the Bright Angel Trail, only five or so would come back to the next meeting. I loved being with those people, the core group, more than anyone else in the world. We didn't just goof around; we were kind of on a mission, just to see where we could go, to see what we could do. We would climb if we had to in order to get somewhere.

We really enjoyed the beauty. It wasn't like we sat around and talked about how beautiful it was, but we all knew it. We all shared it."

There are several obstacles to roaming around the many canyons that make up the Grand Canyon. The natural ones are the intense heat, the scarcity of water, and the sheer cliff formations. When these massive cliffs glow in the ethereal moonlight, it's possible to wonder if the rock is really so solid. Certainly, some explorers have considered these same cliffs less than impassable. One of them is Harvey Butchart, an NAU math professor known for his extensive Canyon hiking, his rediscovering ancient routes, and his trail guidebooks. He wrote about one route that Ellen found. When I asked her about it, she responded in her modest way.

"It was kind of by accident. I was looking for this other way. I'd have to look at a map to remember, but the year before we had gone up that way, so I wanted to find it again. But I ended up going up a different break in the Redwall than the one before.[2] It turned out that there was a little trail construction along there; it could have been an old route. Anyway, I wouldn't want to say that I'd discovered a route, it was just a fluke. I was actually lost, and I had these other people with me who knew less than I did, so I ended up being the one to make a couple of decisions."

Although she credits a former boyfriend, a dory boatman, with starting her working on the river, her first river trip was with a member of the hiking club: in 1973, she went along as a swamper with her friend George Billingsley. "The river trip was great. After all that hiking in the Canyon, it really tied

2. Redwall is a 500-foot limestone cliff formation.

everything together. I hadn't quite visualized how it was all connected."

Ellen started cooking for Grand Canyon Dories in the summer of 1974, after she received her bachelor of fine arts degree in ceramics. On river trips, boatmen usually cook as well as run boats, but not at Grand Canyon Dories. They hire cooks. The cook was generally the boatman's girlfriend. They didn't really get paid back then, and it wasn't an easy job—they were busy every morning, every lunch, and every night. Still, it was a way to be on the river, in the Canyon, and with your friends. Ellen said that "if it hadn't been for my boyfriend and the wonderful group of dory people, I might not have kept doing it."

But the cooks did quite a bit of rowing and often took over a sick or injured boatman's dory. "I picked rowing up fast, and it was fun to do and stuff, but never in my wildest dreams did I think I would ever be a boatman with Dories." For one thing, Ellen thought rowing would require a lot of strength, and for another, "I think I didn't want to have to push myself to the point where I was challenged, to where I might make a big mistake. I didn't like that responsibility so much. But I started getting encouragement from the guys, saying, 'You know, you rowed that really well.' At the same time I was realizing I could row, they were kind of realizing that maybe women could do this. It wasn't like anybody had ever really thought of it before, I don't think."

The cooks also rowed rafts on the spring and fall training trips, and in a few years, the company started bringing a raft along on commercial trips as an extra baggage boat. Ellen rowed one of these rafts quite a bit. She and her boyfriend rowed dories some on the Green River, and then, in about 1979 (she's not sure when exactly), Ellen rowed her first Grand Canyon dory. "Some people were added on at the last minute, so they needed another boatman. It was an opportunity. I've got to give credit to those guys—all the boatmen. They were all for it.

"I have things that one of them, Regan Dale, said to me that I still remember. If I hit a rock or flipped on a trip and felt bad, he'd always say, 'Just remember, if that's all that happens to you, you're lucky.' "

Ellen passes on the same support that she received. Lori Cooper, the second woman to row a Grand Canyon dory, remembers, "Ellen is wonderful. She is really supportive of everybody at all times. She was on my first trip where I was really nervous and she'd tell me, 'Well, all you can do is the best you can do.' "

Even when Ellen's not there, her calm magic is still reassuring, according to another boatwoman, Ote Dale. "I know that she stands at the top of rapids and that she studies where she's going to go. She'll study where everybody else is going to go too, but she does her own run. She really goes to school. I don't know if Ellie calms herself, but she calms me. I gain strength from visualizing her."

Ellen, like a lot of boatwomen, learned that she could row without being six feet tall and muscle-bound. She learned to maximize technique—to look way ahead, to use efficient angles, to have proper timing, and to always be observing the water. "Ellen is precise and subtle," said one dory boatman. "I remember watching her run House Rock. To make the cut right, I would normally get out in the middle and start cranking on my oars. She'd just float down in, take a few precise strokes and end up in the same place. She changed the way I row."

Regarding strength, Ellen says, "I don't have any problem admitting that I'm not as strong as the guys. For me that's a fact, an obvious fact. Maybe it's because the river is so big and so powerful, that when we're out there together, we are more alike than we are different. Whether you're a hundred pounds or two hundred pounds, you still have to work with the river to get where you want to go."

There's a wonderful kind of strength that a guide develops from carrying passengers. "Whether I feel good or not, I have to come across that way," Ellen said. "I won't go into gory details about where my mind has been the day before or that this is the worst stage possible to run Crystal. I may tell my people something like, 'Crystal is a big rapid. It's really difficult and I need all of your attention. I need you to be with me in your mind.' But I won't actually tell them that I've visualized being hung up and crushed on the Rock Island or something, or that I'd like to tie the boat up and leave. To the people in the boat, I have to maintain this confidence, and because I have to come across that way to them, it gives me more confidence. There's a fine line between faking it and actually being that person."

Ellen tried the same "faking it" technique when she felt nervous about teaching a ceramics class. She pretended she really had something to offer the students, and of course, found out that she did. She's devoting more time now to her art, producing a few shows and opening up a studio in Flagstaff. Her clay sculpture is organic and whimsical, yet strong. "One of the things I like about working with clay is that, after I fire it, it gets real solid, like sedimentary clay turning into hard metamorphic rock. I always thought that was neat—doing a process similar to what the earth does, and did in the Canyon two billion years ago.

"But I'm not trying to pretend that I'm making a sculpture that's as beautiful as what I've seen, like some sand dune that's just been blown a perfect way. I may see something and really like feeling and touching it, but I don't take pictures of it or take it home or anything like that. But later, it might come out in something I'm doing. I don't directly see the influence of the Canyon, but I think when you create, it comes out of your whole history."

Even though ceramics is becoming her main focus, every summer she goes back into the Canyon. The people she works with are a strong draw.

"I can't say what it is that makes them different, but down there . . . everybody's real. I'm not sure if I can really explain that. Maybe it's that we're just who we are there more than any other place. After fifteen years worth of river trips with the same people, there's really a huge bond. It's strange, though, because it just seems to be that and nothing else. But it's so strong and it's so deep.

"There's a group of maybe six or eight of us who, over the years, have done a couple of trips a summer with each other, but we don't really stay in touch otherwise. And it's not that I want to or I think I should. It's just that it's okay the way it is. I know that when I come back the next year, or even if it's not for a few years, it'll be the same.

"When I'm on the river, I know that the people I'm working with will do anything for me. They'll save my life. It's that kind of thing. I mean, we all know. We're always watching out for each other. It's just this sort of unspoken support. There's no question that it's there. Even if we might be mad at each other, we still know that when the chips are down, when there's a problem, we're going to be there for each other.

"And maybe just the simplicity of being in the Canyon

brings us back on track—sleeping on the ground underneath the stars, waking up when it's light, going to bed when it's dark. I really like the sound, in the sense that there's absolutely no car noise, none of that stuff. It's almost like you get the feeling that this is the way it's supposed to be. This is the real world and the other world is the phoney world that we all live in and we all function in. But to get back to the way it really is, the way it's supposed to be—your whole being recognizes that, and there's an overall feeling of peace."

And if you happen to be rowing a wooden boat, there is also a unique feeling of joy. When river guides describe a past rapid run, it doesn't take long before their eyes start sparkling, and they are back on the river. The listener becomes the vehicle they ride back to the water. But the women who row dories get more than a gleam in their eyes. They get special smiles, and then their voices actually take on a lyrical lilt, like a dory riding up and over the waves. Ellen was no different. At least, not after she got over her hesitancy to talk about how she felt about dories as compared to rafts. She didn't want to give the impression that she thought dory boatwomen were superior oarswomen. But dory guides definitely accomplish something each time they row their rigid quarter-inch plywood boats through the Grand Canyon in one piece, without crashing on a rock or flipping. It is what they refer to as a "golden trip."

Ellen was also reluctant to talk about flipping, because she didn't want people to think dories flipped all the time—which they don't. But she did say, "If I hear the cans in my hatches slide, I pretty much know that I'm going over. The next sound is quiet because I'm under water. Usually, though, they're like a kayak in that you can brace downriver into the biggest waves and not go over. That means everyone, including the boatman, is holding onto the gunnel and leaning downstream. Still . . . sometimes it's just not your day. But with a dory, getting the boat back over can be so easy.

"I have everybody primed for if we're upside down. I climb up on the bottom and get everybody up there. Then I pull the slack out of my flip straps that are tied to the gunnel. We stand on one side of the boat, lean back, and right it.

"I think just about every time, except for maybe twice, I and whoever has been with me in the boat have been able to right it before people even row out to rescue us. There's been some flips where I really felt like I hardly got my head wet. It was fast—the boat was coming over, and I was on the gunnel. Then it was over, and I was on the bottom. I mean, it's great, and it makes the trip for the people. As much as I hate to flip, if nobody's hurting, they'll remember it forever. But I'm always really glad, too, that nobody does get hurt because I know the potential.

"But, mostly, you hit something straight and pushing into it with a rigid dory—that's what's so wonderful about them—they just punch right through there. They can still get stalled and surfed, and they can get turned and stuff too," and Ellen's voice lightens as she rides downriver, "but they're just so neat. You're like a cork—you go up, over, and through . . ."

The last time I saw Ellen on the river she was rowing the "Music Temple," an old dory she acquired from Martin when he sold the company. Most of the other dories were painted with strong reds or bright turquoises. Hers was more subtle—white with a green gunnel. When she drifted closer, I could hear the water slap against her wooden boat. As her dory glided downstream, its white sides reflecting the rippling movement of the river, I had to agree with what Ellen had said: "They're completely different than anything else. Well, they're a boat, they're an actual boat."

CHAPTER 15

James E. Thomas, Jr.

Martha Clark

Martha Clark started working with AZRA in 1978. This energetic woman with straggly blond hair and large blue-green eyes is the embodiment of enthusiasm and fun. Nothing seems to slow her down, not even when her feet are cracked and raw from the mysterious foot rot that has started to plague Canyon guides. Martha is constantly in and out of the water—her hair flattened down around her ears, and her baggy shorts and sleeveless cotton top dripping wet as she climbs back into her boat and dons her cowboy-styled felt hat.

Martha told me, "I don't know how you're going to talk about romance in your book, but you're going to have to because it's truly part of all our lives down there—and in a big way—because it's an incredibly sensuous environment. Think of how many times you've fallen in love down there, and how many times people have fallen in love with you. It's a place we shine. We're the happiest in our lives. We're vibrant. We're just so full of life, and not only does that put you in the mood for love, it sets you up for it. People are really drawn to people who are shining, who feel so happy with where they are and who they are and what they're doing and who they're doing it with."

It can't be said any better than that, and needn't be. There is definitely romance on the river, and Martha has had her share of it. Yet her most enduring romance seems to be with the Grand Canyon.

"It was the vastness. I was so in awe that first summer. It was just so huge there was nothing to put it in perspective. Sometimes there still isn't.

"I didn't think I was going to love it as much as I did. I'd hiked in Escalante, Zion, and trekked through Nepal. I'd worked in the Gila, the Sierras, Big Bend, and fished in Alaska. I'd seen the Grand Canyon from the top, but you don't get it from there. Maybe if you stood there a few days, from sunrise to sunset, you'd start to feel its character and depth. I can see why people only spend twelve minutes at the rim; they look down and don't know what to do with it.

"I went nuts my first trip. The river was so much fun, the Canyon was so beautiful, and these people I was working with were blowing me away. I was in love with a couple of different boatmen." She laughed. "But by the end of the trip, I'd narrowed it down to one.

"I remember one day, going up into upper Elves Chasm. We climbed all these big boulders and went to the far fern-covered wall. Then, back on the river, we floated downstream through all that obsidian-like rock, and ran Deubendorff in big water. We pulled in at the bottom, and the dories were there playing with this little inflatable kayak. One boatman and I carried it back up to paddle through Deubendorff. I was terrified. After that, we hiked up Stone Creek, and then the next day we hiked up to Thunder River. It was almost becoming too much for me—it was so phenomenal, almost like overload.

"I started crying when I saw Thunder River. It was wild to me—this blue-green river cascading down through cottonwoods and green willows in the heart of the desert. That was like the culmination of it. Then we ran up Havasu, and I started laughing. It was fairy-tale land, so gentle and beautiful."

Six years before her first Grand Canyon trip, Martha had signed up for an Outward Bound course: a twenty-eight day, January mountaineering trip in southwest Colorado. After growing up in Waukegan, Illinois, and attending college in Minnesota, she was used to bitter cold. "That Outward Bound course was the first time in my life that I was introduced to something I was really excited by. Not only did I have a blast, but I met people not much older than me who were making their livings in the outdoors and loving it. I took a leave of absence from college that semester, and I guess I'm still on leave."

Martha started working as a kitchen helper with Outward Bound and eventually became a course director. Outward Bound taught her to deal with fear and gave her confidence facing new situations. "Sometimes I can't even call it fear anymore. It's not that I don't get butterflies or worry, but it's not incapacitating. In fact, it's something that I almost get energy from."

Martha was an exuberant twenty-five-year-old representative from Outward Bound on her first AZRA trip, a chartered paddle trip full of diplomats from various countries. Even though Martha was an assistant, the boatmen made her captain most of the rapids. "Those guys," she chuckled, ". . . they decided to put me through my own Outward Bound experience. I'd been in a canoe before, but I'd never paddled a raft, I'd never rowed."

"After the Outward Bound paddle trips, I went on a regular commercial AZRA paddle trip. We did the same things on both. We took them up places like Silver Grotto, where we did all these boulder problems, swam through the pools, and froze our asses off. We went on this adventure, we were having fun. In Outward Bound, you'd go on the same adventure but there was a little bit of—we're supposed to be pushing ourselves, we're supposed to be suffering a little bit. On commercial trips, there was this freedom in not being responsible to facilitate a growth experience (even though it happens on practically every trip), and that lightened the load for me."

Although she thought Outward Bound was an incredible program, she decided to work on the river. Even now, she laughs hard, making the veins in her neck stand out, as she describes her decision. "I thought, where have I been? I've been carrying a sixty-pound pack around the mountains and these guys," her words almost disappear in laughter, "these guys have been going down the river, rowing boats and hiking up these incredible side canyons carrying only little day packs, and then going down and drinking piña coladas at night!"

It wasn't long before Martha was leading river trips. Most guides who started in the 1970s feel that the clientele has slowly changed. Because of magazines, videos, books, former passengers, and advertising, people come with more expectations and a little less sense of mystery and adventure. Martha said, "These days, you can get a guide book for everything telling you what to expect, where to go, how to find it." Does that change how Martha runs a trip? "No," she said, laughing.

Some of Outward Bound's principles may have influenced the way Martha leads a trip. You are definitely not on a scenic bus tour, but on an adventure. "It's true," she says, "I do tend to hike their brains out. I think people like to be pushed. I think they like it physically, emotionally, and spiritually. It's exciting. It makes the trip more rewarding to me. I guess I feel personally responsible for people having the best possible time they can."

And people do have fun with Martha. The company office is stacked with letters from passengers saying how much they loved her contagious fun and support.

"Martha, with her goddamn, innocent doe eyes," a co-worker said, "she has a real gift with people. She takes them past where they think their edge is. I've been on hikes where people stopped and didn't want to go any further. I'd try to encourage them to go on. I'd give them my best shot, and finally I'd leave. Then later, here comes Martha with them, and these people are just elated. She has cards to play that I didn't even know were in the deck. It's one of her skills, her art forms."

It's not only hiking Martha encourages. It's other fun too—jumping off cliffs into bubbling pools, swimming into fern-covered caves, or just generally being silly. Wild, high-spirited, and intelligent, Martha is an expert at bringing people out. As Suzanne Jordan put it, "Observant, sensitive, and patient, we draw people out of themselves. Uninhibited, we allow their inner personalities to flow." One of a guide's greatest rewards is watching people drop their barriers, enjoy each other, and remember how to play.

Being with people and being outside are two of the most important things in Martha's life—that and maybe telling stories. Her eyes gleam and her hands move as she keeps passengers entranced with story after story. Her voice is either emphatic or on the edge of hilarity, punctuated with rapid-fire chuckling. Every so often a phrase will almost disappear into an excited, hoarse squeak, as if her voice is about to give out.

As we walked along a dirt road by her home in northern New Mexico, she told me about one of her trips.

"It was sort of a vision-quest charter," she said. "One night we were going to have a whole evening of 'celebrating womanhood.' Before we started, a bunch of women from twenty-five to seventy years old were taking a bath at Fern Glen. We had walked to the other end of camp. All the guys were back cooking dinner.

"So we're all taking baths, and for one, I thought it was amazing. How few times have I just been naked running around the planet? I mean, not very many times for being thirty-seven years old. But I looked around and saw that most of those ladies had never stood on the earth without any clothes on. And here these women were all just going nuts. They didn't care about how they looked or if they had fat asses or big bellies. They were all just having the greatest time running around naked. In fact, they were having so much fun, I got them to have this peeing contest. And here were these women lined up—I mean, women like your mother—lined up on the beach with their legs spread like this, seeing how far they could pee. It was great!"

So what does Martha do after a summer filled with action, laughter, and fascinating people? It's the question guides are asked most often: What do you do in the winter? Some run small businesses, some go to school, some work seasonal jobs. Martha knits, sews, and plays music, all the domestic things she doesn't have time for during her eight-trip season. She also cross-country skis, hikes, and goes on private river trips. Just because it is winter doesn't mean she stops "pursuing nature."

And she cooks. Martha loves to cook—in the rain, in blowing sand, it doesn't matter. On commercial river trips, she's in her glory when she's whipping out some epic meal. But when it comes to serving dinner, her pride in cooking doesn't prevent her from hiding a black plastic rat in the serving bowl.

Her meals are worth waiting until dark for, which people often do on her trips because they pull into camp late, tired, and happy from all the fun hiking. As Martha says, "You can sleep when you're dead."

You can also be dry when you're dead. When captaining a paddle boat, Martha's voice is usually hoarse—worn out from yelling at her crew, trying to be heard over the roar of the rapids as she urges them into the biggest waves she can find.

She laughed, "I don't really think people are stupid. They can see. They figure it out and don't come with me if they would like dry runs. Even when I row on a winter private trip, it's really hard for me to miss the biggest wave I can find. It makes me laugh to get hit by water. I have respect for the river, but for me, some of my favorite rides are the wildest rides, the outrageous rides, to be right on the edge and not flip. I mean, they're a lot of peoples' favorite rides.

"I love rowing, but I still love to paddle, even though ruddering is harder on my body, and sometimes I truly lose my voice. There's just this spirit, and the energy at the bottom of a rapid—there's nothing like it.

"It's hard to say which is my favorite rapid. I mean, you'd have to consider all the different water levels. I would have to say Sockdolager is one. And Hermit. And Granite is right up there because I feel the water has so much power over the boat and me. I like it because it's unpredictable; I can't say for sure what's going to happen. I feel like the river takes me in its hands. I don't have a lot of control. It's scary a little, but I guess maybe I like being a little scared. The unknown—that's pleasure, pure pleasure. Now I'd have to say in Crystal the unknown isn't always pure pleasure. I have some history there.

"You know, you scout a rapid, and it could be a really scary level and you're not really enjoying the whole process," she chuckled. "It's almost the hardest looking at it. And then going back to your boat, making sure everything's tied up, tightening your life jacket, and rowing out of the eddy, is still hard. But once you're approaching the tongue, you just lose everything. You're just focused on the river and what you have to do. Life becomes really simple. And it's so cool."

Then Martha's lips pursed and her jaw jutted out slightly in a way that meant a story was coming.

"I remember rowing Crystal with Moley [another boatman] on high water. It was, whatever, 60,000 or 70,000 cfs. We were walking our passengers, and all the boatmen were going through with each other to help high-side and bail. I was going, 'Yaaaaah, Moleeeeeeee'; he was right on the money. He was just so focused doing the right cut and practically on the rocks, running over bushes. It couldn't have been better. And I'm going 'Yah, yah, all right, Moleee! All right!' And then I went, 'Oh, shit.' We were on the right shoulder of the Crystal hole. The wave broke on us and surfed us to the left, and we hung there.

"Suzanne was watching from shore and said she'd never seen a boat stay so long just suspended and not flipping. Moley fell off, and I grabbed onto him. He was on the downstream side of the boat hanging like a sea anchor, and I was hanging on to him, so we were high-siding. But it was the grace of God that let us through, you know what I mean.

"I pulled Moley in the boat, and *we'd just made it through the Crystal hole*! Moley's shorts were down around his ankles, and the boat was full of water, and we were so happy. We were about to eat it on the Rock Island, but we were so happy. We were alive! And I was in hysterics because Moley, with his shorts around his ankles and his little white ass, Moley was just flopping around in the bottom of the boat like a big fish."

Martha could hardly breathe, she was laughing so hard telling this story.

Is there a penalty for all this fun? Maybe. It's a little hard to stop doing it, and everything else can seem so boring. But Martha says it best: "If I died tomorrow, I'd feel like my life has been out-of-sight."

CHAPTER 16

Breaking into the Current

"My way was smoothed by the women who'd gone before," said dory guide Elena Kirschmer. Certainly, many of the women "who came before" had their way smoothed by men—a few outfitters and crews as well as fathers, brothers, and mates. But for some women river guides or want-to-be guides, it has not been easy trying to break into this predominately male profession. These women had to balance their passion for working in the Canyon against their frustration in facing prejudice. Quite a few boatwomen said it was the first time in their lives they had encountered sexism. Those who worked with an open-minded crew or mate had a relatively easy time of it, but not all the outfitters and crews were the same. Because of these company differences, the hiring and accepting of women as Grand Canyon river guides has continued to evolve.

"None of our crew wanted a woman," one boatwoman said. "They told the owner that, but he wanted one. Boy, I cried every night down there." When asked why she stuck with it, she said, "I knew the picture by then. Only one company was really hiring women back then and they had a full crew. Where else was I going to go to get a full season rowing in the Canyon? I had wanted to be down there ever since I was a kid. I'm really into people and facilitating the changes that happen for them down there."

A boatman talked about an incident he witnessed when his trip was scouting Crystal in the early 1980s. "Downriver Trips [not a real name] pulled in, and goddamn it, there was this woman rowing baggage. I *never* thought I'd see a woman on a Downriver trip. When they came down to look at the rapid, this woman came up to me and said, 'Look, can you talk to me about this rapid? These guys won't tell me anything. They won't talk to me at all. All they say is, "If you don't want to do it, let us know, and we'll row your boat through." I want to do it, but just, you know, can you tell me something about it?'

"I said, 'Well, sure, I can tell you the things that I think about the most.' But even before we were finished, those guys were yelling at her, 'Come on, let's go. Let's go! Do you want to run it or not?' "

Frustrations familiar to women in many professions—and some familiar to people facing prejudice anywhere—occurred in river guiding. There were women swampers and assistants who watched less-qualified men get their own boats. There were women swampers who lost their tickets downriver when their relationships with their boatmen boyfriends fell apart. There were women guides who dealt with surly boatmen whose egos had been bruised because their romantic advances were rejected. Several women felt that having a boyfriend or husband eliminated potentially uncomfortable working situations. There were women guides who wanted to lead but were told, "Women don't lead trips." Women who did lead trips often watched the lead boatmen from other trips walk right past them and ask their male swampers where they were planning to hike or camp that day. There were women who felt that, when they began to lead or express their own ideas, they locked horns with the male guides. Some felt their ideas were totally ignored until a man suggested the same thing.

Of course, some of the difficulties women experienced while breaking in had less to do with prejudice than with personality dynamics—whether it was fun for the crew to work together. Also, as one female motor guide who had experienced quite a bit of animosity said, "It shouldn't go unmentioned that women had a hard time, but I also feel that there were men who had a hard time."

It seemed particularly hard for women to break into running the big motor rigs. One boatwoman said, "People discouraged me, saying women didn't have the necessary strength to lift the heavy equipment, particularly changing a spare motor quickly. This argument scared me away for several years, something I feel resentful about now. I later found out I could lift the motor as easily as many men—I'd just never had the chance to try. And in an emergency, with a boatload of ten to fifteen people, there were plenty of hands to help out anyway. When I eventually gained my own boat, I was told, 'This should be a feather in your cap. Not many women can run motor boats.' While I appreciated the praise, I felt sad because I knew a lot of women could handle the job."

There's no doubt that women changed the dynamics of a river crew. Men who wanted more of an old boys' club atmosphere resented the intrusion. It is an easy thing to have your self-esteem wrapped up in adventure guiding. One boatwoman said, "You had to earn their respect without stealing their thunder. In my case, we had very different styles. The guys really thrived on being heroes and would increase the distance between themselves and the ordinary mortals." One male guide said, "I do think women force men to be one way or another—either they ease up and act more caring, or they turn into jerks. But the guys I knew loved having women on the crew. Women are just as much a part of life's adventure as men."

Because many boatwomen felt they were representing all women—both to the crew and to the passengers—some women guides were extra critical of themselves. As Ellen Tibbetts said, "There was this feeling that if we made a mistake, it would be perceived that it was because we were women, not because we were human beings." Some boatwomen believed that when passengers saw a man flip, they assumed that it must really be a tough rapid. But if a woman flipped, passengers thought she really screwed up. Not everyone felt this way. Marilyn Sayre remarked, "I watched men make tons of mistakes, so I never felt I had to prove myself."

Interestingly, a few boatwomen felt that they themselves were extra critical of potential women guides, either to protect the reputation of women on the river or just to protect themselves. One boatwoman said, "I was struggling so hard to get a foothold that I was kind of protective and jealous. I was easily threatened at that point by other women on the river just because my own position seemed so tenuous." Her fears weren't only in her imagination. Another boatwoman said, "I asked our owner why we didn't hire another woman on our crew. He looked at me and explained, 'Because we already have one.' (Another guide added, 'We don't need another woman—too much estrogen.')" As Liz Hymans had said, sometimes there was only room for one "wild card."

A few early boatwomen remember passengers avoiding their boat at Lee's Ferry. Even recently, there have been passenger-related sexism incidents. One example of a guest with an attitude problem occurred when AZRA's Ginger

Hinchman wrapped her boat on a midstream rock in Crystal Rapid. As the boat hit, a woman in the back washed out. Ginger, stuck on the rock in the roaring rapid, could only watch as the woman floated downstream through the Rock Island. Ginger saw another guide, who was unaware that a passenger was in the water, pull his boat into an eddy upstream to help get her boat off. Ginger said, "He said he could feel me, it was like I hit him—so he turned to look at me. I pointed at his boat and then I pointed downstream. He saluted. It was like, yes ma'am, I'll go get her."

Hours later, after Ginger's boat was safely off the rocks, one passenger ranted about suing the company for letting a woman be in charge of a boat. The other passengers told him to shut up.

Assumptions about women on the river can take many forms. Ace mechanic Karen Katzen (a lead guide for Wild River Adventures) smiled at how some male passengers act when there is motor trouble. Karen said, "Once, while everyone was cooking dinner, I was out there trying to fix my motor. I'd been there for about an hour when this passenger came out to help me. The first thing he asked is if I had checked the spark plugs, which is number one on your list to check if your motor's not firing. It's like asking if the appliance is plugged in."

Passengers at pretrip meetings sometimes assume that any female crew member is a cook. Karen said, "I'd get a kick watching their faces when I was introduced as the lead guide."

Another classic assumption is that women will take the most conservative routes through rapids. One exception is Carol Fritzinger, a solid, sun-streaked blond with light brown eyes. Fritz has been working in the Canyon since 1980 and leading trips since 1984. She has freelanced for various outfitters and currently runs trips for Expeditions/Grand Canyon Youth Expeditions.

On a National Park Service boatmen's interpretive training trip, a group of us stood on the hot black rock above Lava Falls trying to decide how to run it at that particular water level—should we run down the right side, through the biggest waves, through the heart of it? Or should we try for the elusive bubble line, hoping to work left of the main wave train? We watched a few boats run through first. One of them was Fritz, and she did a perfect dance down the right side. Everyone said, "Yeah, let's do that." Of course, most of us who tried to "do that" ended up swimming. After my own flip and washing-machine spin flush through Lava, Fritz hauled me into her boat and then, grinning, reached into her cooler and offered me an ice-cold beer.

On Fritz's next trip with the Park Service, the leader told her, "I don't care what you do, but you're going last. I don't want anybody to follow you."

Fritz speaks in a slow, low voice that sounds like she is stretching. She seems to breathe her words in for emphasis. Although Fritz likes getting "clobbered" by waves, she's not into flipping. "I've only flipped twice in my career, and if I never flip again, I'll be proud of that. But I'm out there to get the most out of a ride. I want to take people *boating*."

There may always be occasional passengers who are a bit hesitant about a woman "taking them boating." (That's when it's fun to play the old switcheroo, preferably the morning before a big rapid. The nervous passenger is contentedly tying his or her day bag onto some brawny boatman's rig, when all of a sudden the woman guide jumps on the rowing seat. The passenger pales and mumbles, "Oh . . . uh, is this your boat?") And there will always be the ladies who prefer to be rowed downriver by a bronzed male river god, or the older gentlemen who feel awkward when a woman is in charge. But, overwhelmingly, passengers are very happy to have female guides. In fact, today they're usually rather ho-hum about it. As Sue B predicted, the day has come when we are not considered so special.

Where I once worked almost the whole season with only male crews, now AZRA is unlikely to have fewer than two female guides per trip. In fact, a number of trips put on the water with a higher ratio of female to male guides. With few exceptions, boatwomen in all the companies said they love working with other women. Martha Clark said, "When there's two women—well, there's another woman to relate to, to 'hag out' with. If there's only one woman, the people think you're special, and that heightens the perspective of the guides being different and separate from the passengers." On all-women charters or all-women crew trips, there can be a special co-operative and supportive spirit. Because it was rare to do all-women adventure trips, the first ones were exciting. There was a feeling of yes, we *can* do this ourselves!

Maybe men aren't necessary to pull off a river trip, but most of us prefer the fun of working with them. One fairly new company tries to have an equal number of men and women guides on its trips. The company was founded on a 1987 Wilderness World trip, when Edie Schniewind, a passenger from New York, found out that the company was for sale. Edie had no experience running rivers, but the next year she bought the company and renamed it Canyon Explorations. In recent years, her company has provided a welcome place for women to work as Grand Canyon guides. In earlier years, AZRA had the reputation as *the* company that welcomed women onto its river crews.

AZRA's owner Robert Elliott said, "Women on trips add

so much in, you know, that usual dimension of softness." People have said how nice it was that the women on our crew were "still charming, still feminine," a comment that could be considered somewhat presumptuous or sexist. But Hilde Schweitzer, who rows for Outdoors Unlimited, said something similar: "AZRA was wonderful with women—Martha, Suzanne, and who's that little tiny girl? Lorna? They were neat to aspire to be like, that maybe you didn't have to be macho and look like a guy and act like a guy to be competent."

Of course, no single company has a corner on femininity in the Canyon, and when I think of the AZRA boathags, my first image is not of feminine "softness," but of women laughing—full-throated, good-humored laughter. And I will admit that sometimes it is downright cackling.

Most boatwomen in other companies would not put up with the nickname "hag." But as Suzanne Jordan said, "It's a term of endearment." I recently learned that hags were once considered women of wisdom and power. In fact, the Greek word *hagios* means holy, and an old English definition of *haggard* is "an intractable, or not easily controlled, person." But to most ears, the term "hag" sounds awful. Ann Anderson, who has rowed since 1981 for OARS, said, "It sounds horrible, like a bunch of old witches." Liz Hymans told me, "Don't call me a hag. I think it's unflattering. There are lots of neat women down there who deserve a word that denotes either a little more accurate description or a little more respect." I asked Liz what term she would like to hear used. Liz grinned and said, "River goddess is perhaps more respectful, but it may be a little inaccurate. Just river guide works fine."

Well, as some philosophers might say, perhaps it is time to reunite the goddess and the hag. Regardless of what title Grand Canyon boatwomen use (and most don't mind being called boat*men*), over the years they have definitely earned respect—as perhaps the following story illustrates.

After the peak of the high water in 1983, two AZRA guides, Drifter and Kevin, were standing on the boulder-strewn shore looking at 24-1/2 Mile Rapid. They had heard that Suzanne and Martha had flipped there a week before, and because the river was still flowing high, they stopped to scout the rapid. Drifter was, by his own admission, "about to make the stupidest remark I've ever made." Although there were huge waves and holes, it looked like there was a simple line through the rapid. Kevin asked Drifter if he saw anything unusual going on in the rapid; Drifter shrugged his shoulders and said, "I don't get it. I think we should just call it Boathag Rapid."

Kevin said, "We both laughed, turned, and walked back to our boats. Well, as we were getting ready to run it, I remember looking downstream and seeing Drifter heading toward the rapid, and then I looked away from him again and paid attention to my own thing: life jackets buckled, drag bag in, boxes closed. I think it's going to be a breeze, but still . . . these two women, these two qualified *people*, had this horrible experience here.

"Then I looked downstream again, and I saw Drifter's oar flashing, like a flag of defeat, surrendering over the horizon. I jumped up and looked and . . . Drifter's boat was upside down."

Eventually, we all learn that the river has ears. To his credit, Drifter felt it was an "honor to become an honorary boathag."

Back in 1978, AZRA ran the first all-women's (crew and passengers) trip through the Canyon. At that time, AZRA barely had enough Grand Canyon–qualified women guides who could run the trip: Suzanne, our boss Jessie, and I rowed snouts; Lorna was the assistant/trainee; and Barbara Thomas came out from California to run the paddle boat. Today, there are more than enough working Grand Canyon boatwomen to run several all-women's trips at once.

In the early 1970s, it was a joy to ride the crest of the first wave of Grand Canyon boatwomen after Georgie. And it is wonderful to watch another generation of women—young women who have grown up hearing river stories in which the storytellers are women and the heroes are heroines. In the late 1950s and 1960s, when Robert Elliott and his sister spent summers with their dad running rivers, his sister never rowed. "It wasn't even a question," he said. "It was just presumed. She organized all the food and did most of the cooking." Four years ago, I was on a commercial trip with Robert and his sixteen-year old daughter, Anthea. She rowed a baggage boat while her dad rode along. On the second day, Martha and I stood on the cliff overlooking House Rock Rapid and watched Anthea as she rowed through her first major rapid. She couldn't hear us—or the many other women before us—but as she crashed through the bottom waves, *everyone* cheered, "All right, Anthea! All right!!"

Epilogue

"Every spring, it starts to come on me like a fever," one boatwoman said. "I'm daydreaming about it. About getting up early in the morning and going all day long. About rowing my boat, running rapids, hiking canyons, showing people stuff, and changing people's lives. I'll never get tired of taking people to places like Deer Creek Narrows or Beaver Falls. It's the most rewarding thing in the world to watch people's faces. When I'm down there, I'm thinking—this is what it means to be alive, and there's no reason why I shouldn't do this every summer for the rest of my life."

And why not? When Georgie turned eighty she was still running the river. But then again, she owned her own company. Other guides have to come up with a scheme in case we get too old to get hired. Lorna Corson and I have an idea, and maybe some other "retired" boatwomen will join us.

What we will do is get our old bones to Lee's Ferry, hang around in the shade of the tamarisk trees, and watch the young guides rig their spiffy new boats. We might even, sweet old ladies that we are, offer them a few beers. After the stars have come out and the tired guides are snoring snugly in their sleeping bags, we will sneak down to the boats, untie a few, and shove off.

One of the boatmen might wake up to the sound of laughter and oars moving through the water. He will come running down to the edge of the river just in time to see us disappear into the night, floating toward the first riffle. He will alert his pals, who will ask, "Well, did you see who they were?"

"I don't know," he will reply. "They looked like a bunch of old hags to me."

Bibliography

Annerino, John. *Adventuring in Arizona*. San Francisco: Sierra Club Books, 1991.

Daly, Mary. *Gyn/Ecology: The Metaethics of Radical Feminism*. Boston: Beacon Press, 1978.

Lavender, David. *River Runners of the Grand Canyon*. Grand Canyon, AZ: Grand Canyon Natural History Association and Tucson: University of Arizona Press, 1985.

Madsen, Lisa D. "Georgie! Woman of the River." *Wildwater* 7, no. 2 (April/May 1986).

Stevens, Larry. *The Colorado River in the Grand Canyon—A Guide*. Flagstaff, AZ: Red Lake Books, 1987.

Acknowledgments

I want to thank *all* the boatwomen who trusted me to share their thoughts and feelings, especially: Marilyn, Liz, Susan, Suzanne, Becca, Connie, Sue B, Lorna, Ellen, and Martha. Although guiding is a high-profile job, most of these women are very private people. As I began my research, Marilyn learned that she had colon cancer, and asked me to not include her hospital battles in her chapter. In the spring of 1993, Marilyn passed on.

I am grateful to the following boatwomen I talked with, whose stories could fill yet another book: Ann Anderson, Ann Cassidy, Barbara Thomas, Bebe Salazar, Denise Napoletano, Elena Kirschmer, Edie Schniewind, Carol Fritzenger, Ginger Hinchman, Georgia Gloeckler, Helen Hibbert, Leslie Diamond, Hilde Schweitzer, Judy Schmitz, Jane Bernard, Jessica Youle, Jennifer Lawton, Jamie Harper, Karen Kazan, Kenly Weills, Kellie Janes, Kathy Howe, Kim Claypool, Kimmie Johnson, Lori Cooper, Mary K. Allen, Marilyn Davis, Millit Gray, Mary Lou Mowrer, Nancy McClesky, Nancy Brian, Nancy Rivers, Ote Dale, Peggy Bartlett, Pam Quist, Rebbi Gazzaniga, Robin Gray, Diana Snook, Sharon Hester, and Teresa Yates. I'm also grateful to have spoken with two river women who have since passed on, Georgie White and Joy Ungricht.

Without John Annerino saying, in his subtle way, "*Do* it!" I never would have started this project. And I never would have finished without the hours of editing and constant support of my good friends, Mimi Frenette and Becca Lawton. I'm grateful for the editing and/or advice from Ann Marchort, Lynn Matis, Nancy Brown, Jane Freeman, John Annerino, and Janet Visick. And many thanks go to the University of Arizona's editors Amy Chapman Smith and Judith Wesley Allen, the University's reviewers, and all the University production personnel. I appreciated Larry Stevens, David Lavender, Cam Stavely, Katy Ross, Jessica Youle, and Tom Workman answering my questions. Thanks also go to Kevin Johnson, Bob Melville, Terry Brian, Robert Elliott, Dusty Teal, Don Briggs, Allen Wilson, and to Drifter Smith, that endless source of information who patiently explained the workings of the dam.

I want to thank Cam Stavely of AZRA for allowing me flexibility with my river schedule; Rick Quinn for supplying reams of recycled paper; George Crane for providing office space; Bill Karls for his investigative work; and Boyce McClung for his constant warm hospitality in Flagstaff.

I am grateful to all the photographers who volunteered use of their photographs, especially the professionals. My deepest thanks go to my friend David Edwards, whose photos of boatwomen were a constant inspiration as I worked on this book.

I extend profound apologies and thanks to anyone I have inadvertently neglected to acknowledge.

Lastly, my loving appreciation goes to all the people I have floated with and to the River . . . the River . . . the River.

About the Author

Louise Teal is a writer who has been published in *Arizona Highways, Backpacker*, and *Bicycling* magazines.

Teal writes about these boatwomen because she's one of them. She began working as a swamper (assistant motor boatman, as they called it) in 1972. She started rowing commercially in the Grand Canyon in 1974, and in 1978, she led the first all-women's Grand Canyon trip. The next year she worked as the first woman river ranger for Grand Canyon's National Park Service.

This summer, as she's done every summer for the last twenty-plus years, she will be back on the river.